WINTER ARRANGEMENTS

by Mary Gudgeon
and John Clowes

M & J PUBLICATIONS

CONTENTS

First published in Great Britain in 1995 by M & J Publications, The Hollies, Cattlegate Road, Crews Hill, Enfield, Middx EN2 9DW. (01992) 461895
Production services by Book Production Consultants, Cambridge.
Drawings and cover design by Broxbourne Design (01992) 441726
Reproduction services by Shades Litho, Hoddesdon (01992) 441527
Printed by Kyodo Printing Co. (Singapore) Pte. Ltd.

ISBN 0 9509748 6 2

Arrangements by Carol Pritchard, Mary Gudgeon and John Clowes.

For other titles in the series
See inside back cover.

INTRODUCTION

With this colourful and imaginative book anyone can fill their home with attractive flower arrangements to brighten the dull days of winter.

Many traditional Christmas favourites have been included plus some new ideas. Whether you are an experienced flower arranger or just a novice you will find arrangements which should inspire you to action.

For each arrangement throughout the book you will find a list of materials we have used. This follows step-by-step instructions on how the same effect can be re-created. Simple line drawings illustrate the starting points, the scale and the key steps to follow.

On separate pages you will find information on selecting and conditioning fresh flowers and wiring artificial material. We also show how to prepare bases, tie ribbons, add stems and use candles.

Whatever material or style you choose, whether simple or sophisticated, formal or informal you will find inspiration, advice and ideas which can be adapted to your needs.

3

THE MATERIALS FOR ARRANGING

FLOWERS...

The year-round demand for celebration and sympathy flowers has encouraged the flower industry to have a never-ending supply of beautiful blooms on sale.

Even during winter months florists will have plenty of different flowers on display. Some will be seasonal favourites, others will be out-of-season specials. Even garages and roadside retailers offer a wide range.

All will have carnations, roses and chrysanthemums on offer. But if you are after something a little different you should talk to your local florist to see if they could buy the flowers from market.

FOR WINTER

Alstroemeria	Gerbera
Anemone	Gypsophila
Anthurium	Hyacinth
Aster	Jasmine
Bouvardia	Lily
Carnation	Nerine
Christmas rose	Orchid
Chrysanthemum	Rose
Delphinium	Solidago
Euphorbia	(Golden rod)
Freesia	Stephanotis

FOLIAGE...

The rich dark greens and blues of evergreen foliage are the natural foil to bright winter flowers. Foliage from fir, pine, spruce, juniper and yew trees will be important.

The different varieties of holly and ivy allow variations to be used within one arrangement. You should be able to find large or small plain leaves, silver or yellow-edged foliage. Many holly varieties have male and female forms so not all trees will carry berries.

Don't forget the mystical powers of mistletoe or the value of grey-leaved foliage such as santolina or eucalyptus to provide a good background to white flowers.

FOR WINTER

Asparagus fern	Ivy
Cedar	Juniper
Cistus	Leather fern
Eleagnus	Mistletoe
Eucalyptus	Osmanthus
Euphorbia	Pine
Ferns	Ruscus
Fir	Santolina
Garrya	Spruce
Hebe	Viburnum
Holly	Yew

FRUIT & NUTS...

Whether fresh or artificial, apples, tangerines and lemons in Christmas arrangements add a rich and luxurious look . On page 35 we have even used man-made peaches. Chestnuts, walnuts and peanuts will add a contrast of texture. The methods for adding wire stems to nuts is shown on page 15.

Don't forget that the different types of cones produced by pine, spruce and larch are important elements. Collect the cones wherever you see them lying. The seed heads from poppies and teasels are also worth collecting. Garden centres will have exotic seed heads from protea and lotus for sale.

FOR WINTER

Apples	Artichoke heads
Tangerines	Cones
Lemons	Teasels
Limes	Protea heads
Oranges	Lotus
Peaches	Chestnuts
Pears	Walnuts
Grapes	Brazil nuts
Pomegranates	Peanuts

ACCESSORIES...

Candles are symbolic in most festivals and make attractive centres of interest during the dark winter nights. Choose them with care, and buy early for Christmas.

Ribbons are available in a huge variety of colours, widths and finishes. Once again buy early in December for the first choice.

Similarly the baubles, bangles and man-made berries which are sold by garden centres are on display from November onwards. A few sprays of artificial holly with red berries should be in everyones store. Look out for realistic fruit, attractive figures and perhaps a toadstool or two.

FOR WINTER

Candles	Beech twigs
Ribbons	Cinnamon sticks
Baubles	Reindeer moss
Berries	
Bells	

PREPARING THE FLOWERS

Just carrying fresh flowers home from the florist means that they have been out of water for some time. The cut ends will have sealed themselves and when subsequently arranged in a vase or Oasis cannot easily draw up enough water for the flower stem to last its maximum ltime. All material therefore needs preparation at home to prolong the life of foliage and flowers

1. CUT AT AN ANGLE

The idea is therefore to re-cut the stem to open up the waterways again. Use a sharp pair of scissors, a knife or secateurs and cut at an angle of about 45 degrees. Take just half an inch (1.5cm) off at this stage.

Don't smash stems with a hammer. Research shows that this action doesn't help woody stems to absorb water. It is more useful to slit up the length of stem for an inch or so, using sharp scissors or a knife.

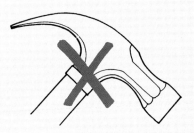

2. STRIP LEAVES AND THORNS

Strip the lower leaves from stems which could decay when under water. Some shrubs such as lilac, veronica, buddleia and viburnum should have all their leaves removed to help prevent the wilting of flowers. At the same time cut off leafy lower branches. Rose thorns can be stripped using scissors to make the stems more easily handled.

3. SOME SHOULD BE HEAT TREATED

Flame Stems which exude sticky material from the cut ends need to be singed with an open flame. Use a candle to seal the ends.

Singe with an open flame; euphorbia, ferns, poppy.

Or Boiling Water Some flowers take up water more readily if the cut stems are given a quick plunge in very hot water. Protect the blooms from steam and dip the ends in boiling water for about 30 seconds. This treatment will also revive flagging rose heads.

Give hot water treatment to acanthus, angelica, buddleia, celosia, clarkia, cytisus, gerbera, hollyhock, lavatera, magnolia, rudbeckia.

4. FILL UP HOLLOW STEMS

Some stems such as delphinium are hollow and quickly dry out. Before giving them a deep, long drink fill the stems with water and plug the ends with a small piece of cotton wool.

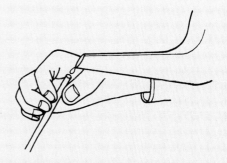

Fill the hollow stems to; delphinium, hippeastrum, hollyhock, lupin.

5. GIVE THEM A LONG DRINK

The tall green vases and buckets favoured by florists are not just for show. They do a useful job in giving cut stems a good deep reservoir for maximum uptake of water. You should do the same. Aim to leave all plant material in deep water for at least two hours, preferably overnight. Tepid water rises to the flower heads much quicker than cold water.

Remember to wash out these containers occasionally with diluted bleach to prevent the build up of algae or bacteria which could reduce the life of your flowers.

Wrap tulip and gerbera stems in newspaper before soaking so that the stems stay straight.

6. TREATING THE WATER

Some people swear by fresh tap water, others add proprietary crystals to extend the life of their arrangements.

These materials, such as Chrysal and Bio Flowerlife work by providing sugar to feed the plant material and algicides to stop the water tubes in the stems from blocking and the water in the vase from smelling.

If you are without these proprietary materials one drop of bleach and a teaspoon of sugar to two pints of water will help to extend the life of the arrangement. Use the solution to soak your foam material or fill the appropriate vase.

CONDITIONING

Probably the most important thing to learn for the prolonged life of an arrangement is the treatment of your material before arranging.

STANDARD TREATMENT

Cut about half an inch (1cm) from each stem. Cut at an angle. Give them a long drink.

African lily (Agapanthus)

Anemone

Anthurium

Antirrhinum

Astilbe

Baby's breath (Gypsophila)

Belladonna lily (Amaryllis)

Bells of Ireland (Molucella)

Brodiaea (Triteleia)

Carnations (Dianthus)

Columbine (Aquilegia)

Daffodil

Decorative onion (Agapanthus)

Freesia

Cornflower

Dahlia

Gladiolus

Globe amaranth (Gomphrena)

Globe thistle (Echinops)

Golden rod (Solidago)

Iris

Ivy

Larkspur

Liatris

Lily

Montbretia

Orchid

Peony

Peruvian lily (Alstroemeria)

Pinks (Dianthus)

Plantain lily (Hosta)

Lady's mantle (Alchemilla)

Love-in-a-mist (Nigella)

Love-lies-bleeding (Amaranthus)

Nerine

Rose

Sea lavender (Limonium)

Saponaria

September flower

Scabious

Solomon's seal (Polygonatum)

Stocks (Matthiola)

Stonecrop (Sedum)

Sweet peas

Trachelium

Tulip* - Wrap in paper

Yarrow (Achillea)

*Also prick stem with a pin below flower head.

SPLIT STEMS

After cutting at an angle, use scissors to cut up stems for an inch or so. This helps woody stems to absorb water. Place in deep water for several hours.

Beech

Birch

Bridal wreath (Spiraea)

Camellia

Chrysanthemum

Eucalyptus

Garrya

Holly

Lilac

Matricaria

Mexican orange (Choisya)

Mock orange (Philadelphus)

Phlox

Rowan (Sorbus)

Senecio

BOILING WATER TREATMENT

Dip stem ends in boiling water for 30 seconds. Remove and place in deep water for several hours.

Angelica

Bear's breeches (Acanthus)

Bellflower (Campanula)

Bouvardia

Broom (Cytisus)

Butterfly bush (Buddleia)

Christmas rose * (Helleborus)

Cock's comb (Celosia)

Cone flower (Rudbeckia)

Godetia (Clarkia)

Hollyhock

Hydrangea

Lenten rose * (Helleborus)

Mallow (Lavatera)

Magnolia

Mimosa

Shruby veronica (Hebe)

Smoke bush (Cotinus)

Sunflower (Helianthus)

Transvaal daisy (Gerbera)

Veronica

Viburnum

Zinnia

*Also prick stem with a pin below flower head.

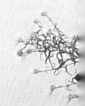

CARE AFTER ARRANGING

FILL HOLLOW STEMS

Fill hollow stems with water and plug with cotton wool. Place in deep water for several hours.

Amaryllis (*Hippeastrum*)

Cow parsley

Delphinium

Dill

Hollyhock (*Althaea*)

Larkspur

Lupin

FLAME SEALED

A candle flame will stop the sticky sap extruding from some stems. After singeing place in deep water for several hours.

Ferns

Poppy

Spurge (*Euphorbia*)

Position the arrangement for best effect, but realise that a cool, shady spot will provide the ideal conditions for the longest life. Bright sunshine and hot radiators are not the best companions of cut flowers, nor are cold draughts.

Make sure that the foam is kept wet at all times. With a large arrangement you may have to top up the water daily. Use an indoor watering can with a long spout so that water can be poured gently onto the top of the florist's foam.

Remember that leaves and flower petals can absorb water from their surfaces. A gentle mist of tepid water over the whole arrangement every day will help to maintain a cool, moist atmosphere.

THE EQUIPMENT YOU WILL NEED

You don't need a mountain of equipment to prepare your flowers, but an efficient pair of secateurs and a sharp pair of scissors will pay dividends.

1. Scissors
Any scissors will do as long as they are sharp. Ones with serrated edges seem to cut stems more easily.

2. Secateurs
For woody stems a pair of secateurs may be useful.

3. Knife
Keep a sharp kitchen knife for cutting foam blocks and stripping thorns.

4. Wire Cutters
An essential tool when adding wire stems to dried and artificial material, or preparing ribbon bows and baubles.

USEFUL EXTRA

5. Fine Sprayer
A hand sprayer is invaluable for delivering a gentle mist of plain water over the arrangement.

THE MECHANICS YOU WILL FIND USEFUL

Don't be frightened of the term 'mechanics' in flower arranging. It only describes the devices and methods which are used to hold flower and foliage stems in position. Here are some of the items you will find useful. On the following two pages you will see how they are used to give you a firm foundation for your flowers.

6. Green florist's foam
Sold under many brand names including 'Oasis' this florist's foam is a vital basis of many arrangements of fresh material. When thoroughly soaked it provides water and holds stems in exactly the same position as when first pushed into the material. It can be obtained in various shapes and all can be cut with a knife to fit most containers.

7. Brown florist foam
For arranging dried and artificial material. This foam will *not* absorb water.

8. Foam anchors
This four-pronged anchor, sometimes called a frog, is used to hold foam or Dri-Hard firmly in the container. The anchor is stuck to the base of the container with Oasis Fix.

9. Adhesive tape
Useful for taping down blocks of foam. Available in white and green.

10. Chicken wire
Useful for larger arrangements where blocks of foam need extra support. Chicken wire which is coated with green plastic is best.

11. Oasis Fix
A fixative material used to secure the foam anchor to the base of the container of your choice. 'Oasis Fix' is a brand name for one of these fixatives but others are just as suitable.

12. Dri-Hard
The best known brand of material which sets hard after a few hours to hold artificial or wired stems permanently in position.

13. Stem wrap
A crepe tape used to bind stems and wires thus hiding the mechanics.

14 Mossing pins
To hold moss firmly to foam.

15. Wires
Stub wires like this are available in various lengths and thicknesses. Choose the right gauge for the job.

16. Glue
A fast-drying, clear glue is recommended for attaching material to wicker rings or to fix wires to decorative nuts.

17. Candle Holders

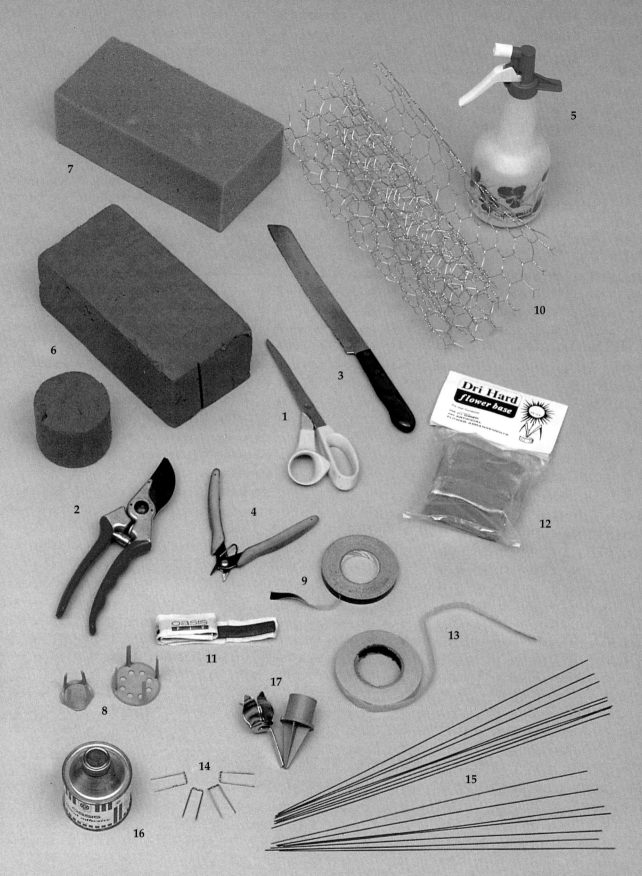

Preparing the Bases and Containers

The Standard Method

1. Find a suitable container or base for the size and shape of the arrangement you have in mind.

2. Push a piece of Oasis Fix or other adhesive onto the flat base of the anchor and push down firmly onto the floor of the container. Use more than one anchor for large blocks of foam.

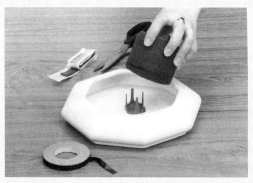

3. Push the wet foam block onto the anchor.

4. Use adhesive tape from one side of the container, over the top of the foam and stick to the other side of the container. A cross of tape will ensure the foam is held firm.

Variations

Vase
Place a pin holder into the bottom of the vase. Alternatively put some chicken wire into the mouth of the vase to support the stems.

Wicker Basket
Line wicker baskets and anything porous. Either use a polythene bag or a plastic tray as the waterproof base.

THE PEDESTAL METHOD

Find a waterproof container which will hold two blocks of Oasis and sits comfortably on the pedestal base.

1. Fix four anchors into the base of the container using Oasis fix or other florist's clay.

2. Take one foam block previously soaked in water and push this onto the anchors at the back of the container in a vertical position. Cut the next block slightly shorter and position this at the front.

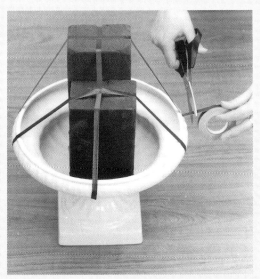

3. Use florist tape from one side of the container, over the top of the foam, and stick it to the side of the container. A cross of tape will ensure the foam is held firm.

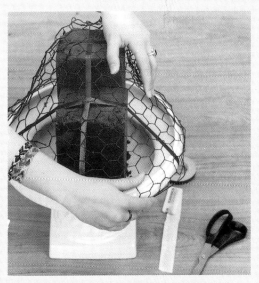

4. Use chicken wire or other mesh to go over the foam. Wire into position under the rim.

TECHNIQUES OF WIRING

Cones, dried and artificial flowers and foliage are not always available with a suitable stem. By adding a wire stem you can lengthen short stems and provide a method for firm positioning of any material.

DOUBLE LEG WIRE

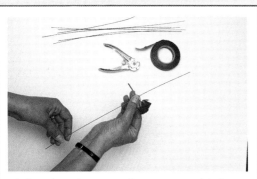

1. Lay the wire across the stem, one third on one side; two thirds on the other.

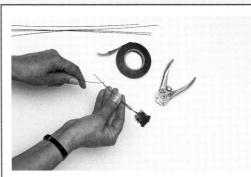

4. Continue to twist this wire down to the bottom.

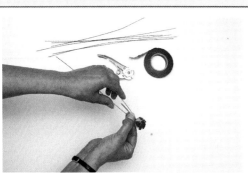

2. Bend the wires into a hairpin shape.

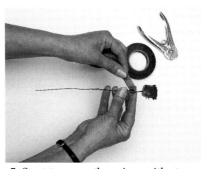

5. Start to cover the wires with stem wrap starting at the flower end.

3. Grip the bend of the wire with thumb and forefinger and twist the longest wire around the stem and the short wire.

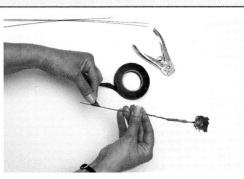

6. Completely cover with stem-wrap and cut stem to length.

WIRING CONES

WIRING NUTS

1. Slip a stub wire between the scales of the cone as low down to the base as possible.

2. Pull wires down on opposite sides of the cone towards the stem of the cone.

3. Twist the longest wire around any stem and the other wire.

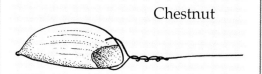

Chestnut

Push a wire through the nut from the curved side. The wire is best pushed through at about a quarter of the way from the base to the point. Bend the wires until they are parallel and twist the longest wire around the other wire.

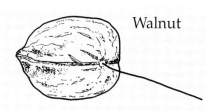

Walnut

Push a wire into the walnut at the base end. The wire will go in easily if you find a central point along the seam which joins the two halves. Once in position put a blob of glue at the point where the wire meets the nut.

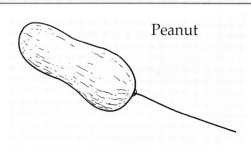

Peanut

Gently push a wire into the end of the peanut shell. Once in position put a blob of glue at the point where the wire meets the nut.

TYING RIBBONS

Below is shown the method for tying a bow with two tails. On the right, the method if four tails are required. The number of loops can be increased at stage 2 below or stage 5 on the right.

DOUBLE-LOOP BOW WITH TWO TAILS

1. Leave enough ribbon from the cut end to make the desired length of tail and pinch the ribbon tightly.

3. Pinch all the riboon together and cut to create the second tail.

2. Bend the ribbon under to create a loop and pinch the ribbon. Make a second loop on the other side.

4. Lay a wire over the centre pinch point and bend one half of the wire to make a double leg.

5. Twist one wire tightly around the other to hold the pinch of the ribbon in place.

DOUBLE-LOOP BOW

1. Cut a separate length of ribbon to make the two extra tails.

3. Pinch the ribbon tightly

5. Make the second loop and pinch the ribbons together. At this stage add further loops if needed.

7. Bend one half of the wire to make a double leg. Twist one wire tightly around the other.

WITH FOUR TAILS

2. Lay the main part of the ribbon over the original, leaving the cut end to make tail No. 3.

MULTI-LOOP BOW

4. Fold the ribbon under to make a loop. Pinch into the centre.

1. Leave enough ribbon from the cut end to make the desired length of tail and pinch the ribbon tightly.

2. Make a single loop, pinching the ribbons together.

6. Lay a wire across the pinched centre.

3. Move around the centre making as many loops as needed.

4. Lay a wire across the pinched ribbon and bend one half of it to form a leg.

8.   Pull loops and tails into a decorative position.

5. Bind the wire tightly around the ribbon and the wire leg.

6. Arrange the loops to form an attractive shape.

CANDLES

While candles can be pushed directly into green foam for fresh material, they cannot easily or firmly be fixed into brown.foam for dried material. Here's what to do.

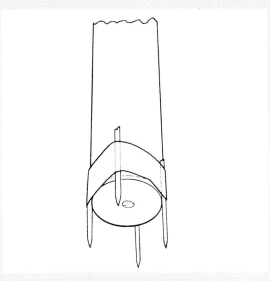

Break two cocktail sticks in half and tape the four pieces to the base of the candle.

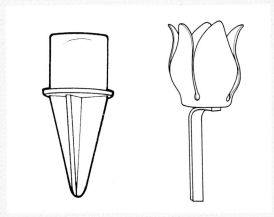

Or use candle holders, either plastic (shown on the left) or metal ones. The candles can then be replace more easily.

BAUBLES

SINGLE BAUBLE

Bend a wire in half and bend one half gently around the bauble 'stem' and around the hanging ring and then firmly around the wire leg. Cover the wire with stem wrap.

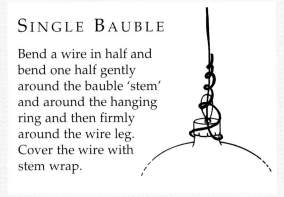

TREBLE GROUP

Push a wire through the hanging rings and make a leg by twisting the wire.

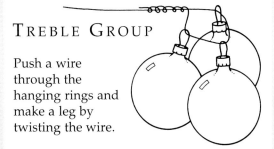

CASCADE

Each bauble is suspended on its own loop of ribbon. For best effect cut the ribbons to different lengths.

When you are happy with the way the baubles hang together, wire the ribbon ends tightly together using the double leg method previously described.

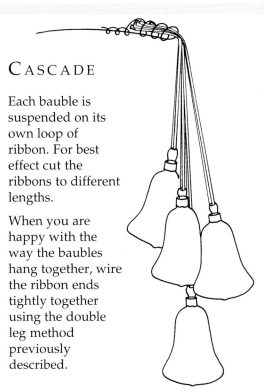

BUNDLES OF STICKS

The use of bundles of twigs or cinnamon sticks is an interesting development to winter arrangements. They need to be in proportion to the overall design and the width of ribbon, if used, and the size of the ribbon loops are important factors to consider.

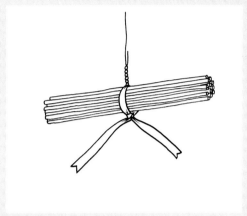

1. Divide the sticks into suitable sized bundles. Wrap a stub wire around the middle and tightly twist one of the wire ends around the straight wire (called a "leg").

2. Select the ribbon and tie around the bundle so that the wire is hidden. The double knot of the ribbon should be opposite the wire stem.

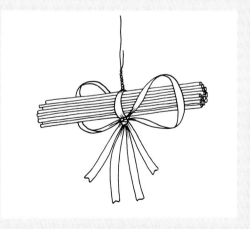

3. Tie a double loop bow (or other variation) as shown on page 16. Position this between the tails of the original ribbon.

4. Use the original tails to tie a double knot to secure the bow to the bundle of sticks. Arrange the four tails attractively and pull bow in position.

HEART OF WINTER

All the traditional favourites are here - holly, ivy, mistletoe, cones, fresh fruit and nuts. Hidden from this view are three more apples, three tangerines and groups of chestnuts and walnuts.

How it is made

Fix two anchors to the base of the dish and push two blocks of freshly soaked Oasis onto the spikes. Trim the Oasis to make a flat-topped cone and then tape over the top.

Start by taping toothpicks to the candle (see page 18) and placing it centrally on the Oasis. Now cover the foam with reindeer moss, pinning it down with mossing pins.

Fig. 1.

Go around the edge of the dish with various pieces of evergreen foliage including holly, ivy, spruce and fir (Fig. 1). To locate the apples, first spike each with a tooth pick and then position them together in a group of three. Use the three lemons, three tangerines and the other three apples in a similar way (Fig. 2).

Now wire the nuts and cones (see page 15), ready to position them into groups around the arrangement.

Between the groups of fruit and nuts use different foliage and some skimmia buds to add textural contrast. Use the lichen covered larch twigs to add a rustic touch.

Finally wire the cinnamon sticks together and tie a decorative bow around each bundle (see page 19). Position in groups of

Fig. 2.

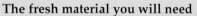
The fresh material you will need
- 6   Red apples
- 3   Lemons
- 3   Tangerines
- 10 Wired walnuts
- 10 Wired chestnuts
- 9   Fir cones
-     Fresh foliage (holly, ivy, spruce and fir)
-     Skimmia foliage and buds
-     Larch twigs
-     Cinnamon sticks for six bundles
-     Red candle

BLUE AND GOLD CANDLES

A little out of the ordinary, but the flowers match the attractive candles and create a simple but stunning arrangement. Try to find candles with a blue and yellow colouring for best effect.

How it is made

Position one anchor at the back of the circular white dish with Oasis Fix or other florist's clay. Push half a block of well-soaked Oasis onto the anchor.

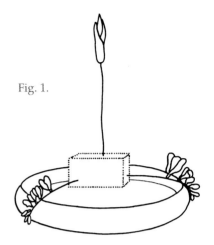

Fig. 1.

Use the sprigs of yellow and gold Eleagnus foliage to cover the edges of the block of foam, then establish the required height of the arrangement with the first iris placed centrally. For best effect use a tight bud.

Now use yellow freesias close to the dish to create the base of the triangular shape and define the proportions (Fig. 1). Point the base line flowers forward to cover the edges of the dish and to give the shape depth.

Use the remaining irises to fill in the triangular shape (Fig. 2), and then bulk out the shape with freesias. Use holly and ivy pieces to establish curves around the base and to hide the Oasis foam.

Position the candles at the front of the flowers to complete the arrangement.

Fig. 2.

The fresh material you will need
- 20 Yellow freesias
- 8 Blue iris
- 5 Sprigs variegated holly
- 5 Sprigs variegated yellow ivy
- 6 Sprigs *Eleagnus pungens* 'Maculata'
- 3 Candles of various shapes - ball, pyramid and column

RED AND TARTAN

The mixture of red carnations with white gypsophila provides a good match with the lampshade. The winning touch is the double loop tartan ribbon which brings all the colours together.

How it is made

Place a plastic bowl, to give a waterproof container, inside a decorative wicker basket.

Position two anchors in the base of the bowl with Oasis Fix or other florist's clay and push on a block of well-soaked Oasis fresh foam.

Start to make a circle of evergreen using the holly and Leylandii conifer foliage together with some flower buds of skimmia (Fig. 1).

Next place three carnations in the centre to give the required height to the arrangement (Fig. 2). Start to create the dome shape using the large carnations around the whole area of the arrangement.

Wire the double loop ribbon bow as shown on page 16 and position this to the front of the arrangement.

Fill in between with Nordman fir and shorter sprigs of holly recessed below the flowers to ensure complete coverage of the foam. Use the spray carnation buds and remaining skimmia heads to complete the shape.

Wire the cones separately as shown on page 15 and place in two separate groups of three. Complete by recessing small bunches of white gypsophila evenly around the arrangement.

Fig. 1.

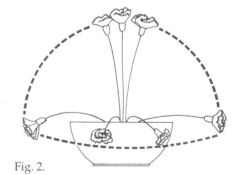

Fig. 2.

The fresh material you will need
20 Large red carnations
15 Stems spray carnations
 1 Bunch gypsophila
 5 Sprigs variegated holly
 7 Pieces Nordman fir
 3 Pieces Leylandii conifer
 7 Sprigs skimmia foliage
 6 Fir cones
 1 Yard tartan ribbon

FATHER CHRISTMAS TOBY JUG

A simple all round arrangement which could be used in any container, but sparkles in this festive Toby Jug. The coppery coloured freesias blend beautifully in this fireplace setting.

How it is made

Cut the block of Oasis to shape and when completely soaked fit into the jug, ensuring at least 3cm (1 inch) of foam shows above the lip of the jug.

Go around the base with eucalyptus foliage to give trailing pieces which fall below the rim of the jug (Fig. 1). Work up with eucalyptus and osmanthus foliage to give a green base to the arrangement.

Fig. 1.

Now set the height of the arrangement with freesias. This should be approximately one and a half times the height of the jug (Fig. 2).

Gradually build up the domed mass of freesias ensuring that the flowers face in different directions but look as if they come from a central point.

Use the remaining eucalyptus foliage in between the freesias and finish off with white September flowers proud of the freesias to give points of interest outside the main body of flowers.

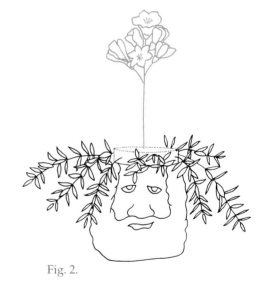

Fig. 2.

The fresh material you will need
20 Antique gold freesias
12 Spikes of September flowers
 6 Buds osmanthus foliage
 2 Branches of miniature eucalyptus

BLUE AND SILVER CURVES

The cool colours of blue and silver in this arrangement epitomise the beauty of ice and snow. By using silk material you will have an arrangement which will be useful throughout the winter.

How it is made

Fix an anchor to the base of the bottom cup and then push on a ball of Dri-Hard.

Define the height of the base arrangement with a bud and flower of Christmas rose in the centre. Use two more flowers to make a curved line coming forward. On the right hand side use oak foliage and silver grapes (Fig. 1).

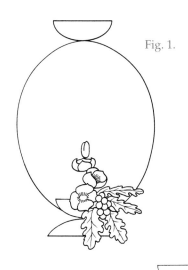

Fig. 1.

On the left hand side use blue campanulas and blue baubles to complete the shape. Varied foliage is used to fill between these main elements. The foliage will balance the width and give a variety of texture (Fig. 2). Add a double-loop ribbon bow (see page 16) towards the back.

Position an anchor in the top cup with Oasis Fix and push on a ball of Dri-Hard. Fit a candle holder in the centre with vertical silver candle.

Start to emphasise the line of the oval with blue spruce stems and hydrangea flowers to the left of centre. Use other foliage and white poinsettias on the right. Fill in the right hand side with three Christmas roses in a curve and three dark campanulas in the centre, pointing forwards (Fig. 3). The silver grapes, blue campanula and a few dark blue grapes complete the shape on the left.

A double-loop bow with four tails provides a visual link between the two arrangements.

Fig. 2.

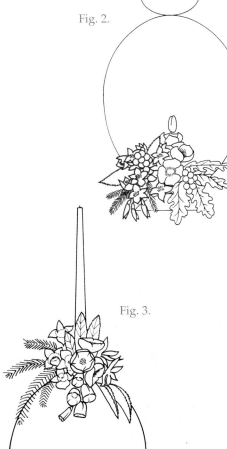

Fig. 3.

The artificial material you will need
- 3 Stems of blue campanula
- 2 Stems pale blue campanula
- 5 Pale blue hydrangea blooms
- 6 Christmas roses with buds
- 2 Stems grey oak leaves
- 2 Sprigs blue spruce foliage
- 10 Small white poinsettia heads
- 7 Sprigs of silver grapes
- 10 Sprigs blue grapes
- 2 Yards of blue ribbon
- 1 Silver candle

COPPER AND CONES

This offset arrangement relies heavily on the contrast between smooth flowers and the harsh angles of cones and twigs. If a copper container is not available then use a rustic wicker basket.

How it is made

Find a large plastic bowl and position a block of Oasis with an anchor. Put the bowl at the left hand side of the copper container and position the handle angled to the left of upright. Fix the candles on the right hand side of the handle to give a central point.

Use the five sprays of alstroemeria (Fig. 1) and the chrysanthemums (Fig. 2) to set the perameters of the overall shape.

Fig. 1.

Fill in with various pieces of foliage. At the back use the leather fern and some holly and spruce to provide a solid background.

Wire each of the bundles of twigs and position them centrally at the front at different angles. Use the broom stems in fairly large bunches with some other foliage to complete the front rim of greenery. Arrange the roses in groups to provide the main points of interest. There are five roses to the right of the candles, pointing to the right, five at the front, pointing forward and the rest used towards the back and left hand side to maintain the colour impact.

Fig. 2.

Finally position the three stems of beech foliage for contrast and then fill the right hand side of the bucket with large fir cones to provide an interesting contrast.

The material you will need
20 Pink roses
5 Stems of spray chrysanthemums
5 Alstroemeria
5 Sprigs holly foliage
5 Sprigs broom foliage
6 Sprigs spruce foliage
3 Stems dried beech leaves
5 Leather fern
7 Bunches of twigs
7 Large cones
3 Copper coloured candles

PLUMS AND CREAM

All the material in this arrangement is long-lasting - either natural seed heads or man-made. The simple white candle could be changed each year to give a different look for different positions.

How it is made

This monochromatic arrangement works well because similar material is positioned close together yet there is a contrast of texture and form within a rich plum colouring.

Fig. 1.

Fill the bowl with Dri-Hard to within 1 cm (1/2") of the rim, and then position the candle holder in the centre. Ensure the candle is truly vertical.

Use spruce pieces close to the candle to hide its holder. Take the three plums and three stems of maroon berry stems and position these to the right of the candle at different levels (Fig. 1).

On the opposite side use the six poppy heads to make a line of colour (Fig. 2). Beside these poppy heads position three sprigs of maroon berry stems mixed with spruce foliage.

Fill in the other two quarters with the gold material. On one side use the gold seed heads mixed with the spiral twigs and gilded foliage which make a good contrast of texture. On the other, fill in with the white rose, gilded eucalyptus and gold balls.

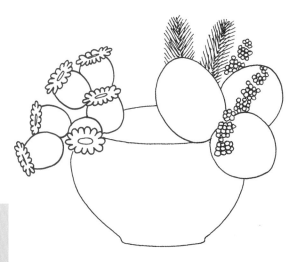

Fig. 2.

The artificial material you will need
- 3 Deep red artificial plums
- 6 Poppy heads painted plum and gold
- 6 Stems maroon artificial berry stems
- 6 Spiral twigs
- 2 Sprigs gold seed heads
- 1 Gilded white rose
- 2 Sprigs gold eucalyptus
- 12 Sprigs spruce foliage
- 3 Gold balls
- 1 White candle

PEACH PERFECTION

This bowl of artificial fruit and foliage relies heavily on the careful selection of material with varying textures but complementary colouring. Grouping creates an informal but stylish effect.

How it is made

Place an anchor in the centre of the bowl using Oasis Fix and then push a large ball of Dri-Hard firmly onto it. Insert the three candles into their holders and place vertically in the centre.

Take six sprigs of fir foliage and space evenly around the edge of the bowl (Fig. 1). The other material will then be used in six blocks.

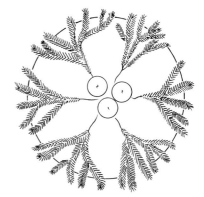

Fig. 1.

Take two large rose hips and position very close to the Dri-Hard. Now place the other rose hips overlapping the lower ones to make a rising step of pink. Use two sprigs of grapes to make a bunch overflowing the edge of the bowl. Use the last sprig pushed up against the candles to give the bunch height and a 3-dimensional look (Fig. 2).

Further to the left use roses and cineraria foliage to create a block and match this with six other roses on the right (Fig. 3).

Now use the five peaches, trailing geranium foliage and the three hydrangea heads to complete the six blocks. Fill in with mistletoe in a line from candle to the outer edge of the bowl.

The last pieces to be put in are the three bundles of twigs which have previously been wired - two between the grapes and rose hips and one between the peaches and hydrangea heads.

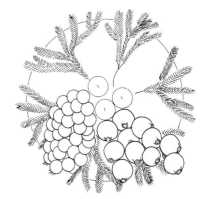

Fig. 2.

The artificial material you will need

21 Antique pink roses
 3 Hydrangea heads
 6 Sprigs of mistletoe
11 Large red rose hips
 5 Peaches
 5 Sprigs trailing pink geranium foliage
 3 Bunches of wooden twigs
15 Sprigs of pine foliage
 3 Sprigs of cineraria foliage
 3 Candles with holders

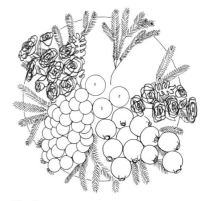

Fig. 3.

TRADITIONAL LANTERN

A simple but attractive arrangement which sits prettily in this window. Bundles of natural twigs give a rustic look to artificial material which blends happily with the wrought iron lantern.

How it is made

Push some Dri-Hard into the base of the lantern.

In your mind's eye create five spokes of a wheel and start by placing a sprig of holly foliage at the rim of each one of these spokes. Make sure that the foliage of the holly overlaps the rim of the base.

Between each holly sprig place some fir foliage so that the mechanics are completely hidden by the greenery (Fig. 1).

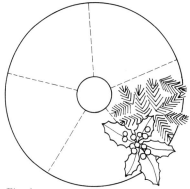

Fig. 1

Recess a poinsettia flower in each of the fir foliage sections, varying the position of the flowers. Some should overlap the edge, while others are positioned nearer the candle (Fig. 2).

Wire the twigs into five bunches (see page 19) and tie each with red ribbon to hide the wire and add a decorative touch. Position beside each poinsettia flower (Fig. 3).

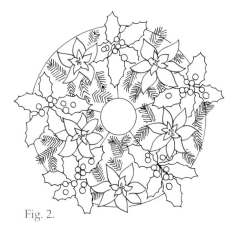

Fig. 2.

Complete the arrangement with two triple-loop bows (see page 16). Position these on opposite sides ensuring the tails are pointing in varying directions, appearing from beneath the foliage.

The artificial material you will need
- 5   Sprigs of variegated holly
- 5   Small poinsettia flowers
- 5   Bunches of thin twigs
- 2   Yards of red ribbon
-     Fir foliage
-     White candle

Fig. 3

DOUBLE RING OF WELCOME

This simple but effective wall decoration can be used year after year and can be positioned indoors, as shown here, or as a welcoming door decoration.

How it is made

Tie the two rings together with a simple loop of ribbon. Position the knot of the ribbon behind the top ring and glue into position. For best results fix the flower and foliage material into position with glue rather than wires.

Start by positioning three sprigs of holly to the left of the main ring. The top point will be halfway up the ring. Then position two more berried holly sprigs on the right hand side (Fig. 1).

There are seven poinsettia flowers at the base of this top ring which should fill some of the internal circular space. One or two of the heads should point downwards and fill some of the space between the rings. Complete this ring with six white Christmas roses which are positioned slightly left of centre (Fig. 2).

In the bottom ring group the remaining poinsettia flowers and some variegated holly foliage on the right, pointing the flowers out and upwards.

Along the base of the ring use three sprigs of holly foliage in a sweeping group and finally glue into position the final three Christmas roses to the left of centre.

Glue the ribbon bows into position. The top one is a six-loop four-tail bow; the bottom one is a four-loop two-tail bow (see page 16).

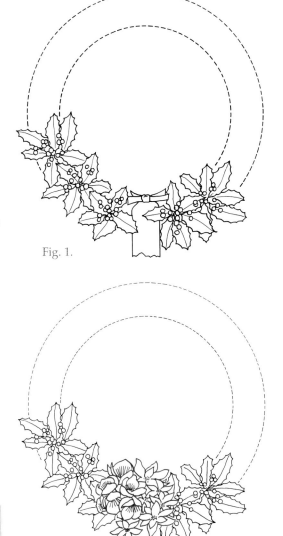

Fig. 1.

Fig. 2.

The artificial material you will need
- 8 Sprigs of berried holly
- 3 Sprigs of variegated holly
- 9 Christmas roses
- 15 Small poinsettia flowers
- 2 Yards of tartan ribbon

LONG, LOW AND SILVERY

This monochromatic arrangement uses grey foliage, white flowers and silver ribbon to create a peaceful contrast against this wooden panelling. Remember it will be lost against a white wall.

How it is made

Secure two foam anchors to the base of the dish with Oasis Fix. Put one at either end. Cut a block of Oasis for fresh material in half and soak both halves. Push half of the Oasis block on each anchor.

Fig. 1.

Start the arrangement by using eucalyptus branches to establish the width and flow (Fig. 1). Fill in with santolina branches creating a long, low crescent shape (Fig. 2).

Complete the basic shape using the variegated euphorbia - one stem at either end and the Leylandii foliage at the same length, sweeping forward, yet touching the base line.

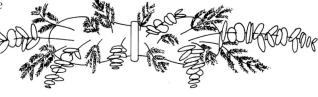

Fill the shape with chrysanthemum flowers, evenly positioning them to the desired shape. Use the spruce foliage to fill in at the back and to create a contrast of texture close to the flowers.

Fig. 2.

Take two yards of silver ribbon and create a loose bow with at least four tails and wire as shown on page 16. Position this in the front centre of the dish.

The fresh material you will need
- 12 Stems white spray chrysanthemums
- 11 Sprigs grey santolina foliage
- 2 Stems variegated euphorbia foliage
- 9 Stems eucalyptus
- 2 Stems Leylandii conifer foliage
- 7 Stems of spruce foliage
- 2 Yards of silver ribbon

Flowers, Fruit and Nuts

This attractive mixture of artificial material provides plenty of different colours, shapes and textures for years of display.   A similar effect could be achieved with fresh material.

How it is made

Fit a foam anchor to the base of the bowl with Oasis Fix or other florist's clay. Push on a ball of Dri-Hard which is proud of the rim. Fit a single candle holder in the centre, making sure the candle is vertical.

Cover the Dri-Hard with green reindeer moss fixed into place using mossing pins to hide the mechanics.

Start by creating a curved arch of nuts grouping similar shells together (Fig. 1). The peanuts will touch the side of the candle.

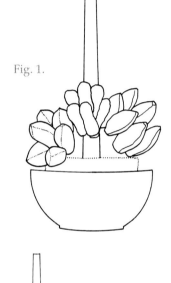

Fig. 1.

Below this arch fill in with variegated holly foliage topped off with ten red poinsettia flowers (Fig. 2).

To the left of the nuts place one sprig of variegated holly foliage and the remaining poinsettia heads. Further round are three sprigs of berried holly, some of which should overhang the edge of the white bowl.

To complete the arrangement use the fruits and further reindeer moss to completely cover the Dri-Hard. Finally use the mistletoe to fill any bare patches which need points of interest.

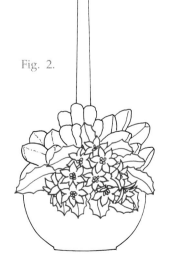

Fig. 2.

The artificial material you will need

12 Poinsettia heads
 3 Sprigs of mistletoe
 6 Wired brazil nuts
 6 Wired peanuts
 6 Wired pecan nuts
 3 Sprigs of berried holly
 3 Sprigs of variegated holly foliage
 1 Artificial lemon
 1 Artificial apple
 3 Artificial pomegranates
    Green reindeer moss
 1 Red candle

FESTIVE PINK ROSES

This is a standard arrangement which is given a Christmas feel with the addition of holly foliage, red baubles and ribbon. Roses in winter are expensive but this arrangement uses them to maximum effect.

How it is made

Find a plastic bowl to sit on the central pedestal of the metal base. Fit a foam anchor to the base of the bowl with Oasis Fix. Soak half a block of Oasis for fresh flowers and push this onto the anchor.

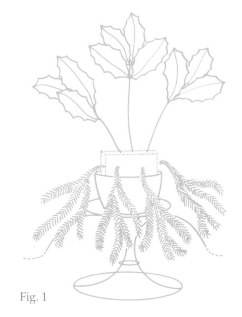

Fig. 1

Start by creating the basic shape with pieces of foliage. Six pieces of spruce foliage pointing downwards around the base will set the bottom line, and three holly stems will set the top perameters (Fig. 1).

Now insert the viburnum heads and spruce foliage to fill out the shape. Use ivy stems, broom twigs and jasmine flowers proud of the main dome of foliage.

Use eight baubles in a cascade (see page 18) and position to the right of centre. There are two multi-loop bows (see page 16) used at the top and half way down the bauble cascade.

The most important element of this arrangement, however, is the roses. Use them so that they dominate the display. At the base they should point downwards and at the top they should be vertical. See that they are positioned around the dome shape without touching each other or being placed in straight lines.

The fresh material you will need
20 Pink roses
     (We used 'Handel' and 'Pink Parfait')
12 Flower heads of viburnum
12 Stems of white jasmine
16 Stems of spruce foliage
 5 Stems variegated holly foliage
 9 Stems of ivy foliage
12 Stems of broom (Cytisus)
 8 Red baubles
     Thin red ribbon

TRAILS OF GOLD

An eye-catching arrangement which is ideal for halls and other areas where flat display space is limited. The yellow and gold colours contrast well with the wood panelling.

How it is made

Buy a wall-hanging Oasis holder (often used as pew-end displays) and fit a well soaked block of foam into the cage holder. Then tape to secure the foam.

Start by using ten pieces of spruce foliage around the edges to create a long oval shape. Use eight heads of golden rod to amplify this shape (Fig. 1).

Start building up the centre with yellow variegated holly. Wire each of the gold baubles as shown on page 18 and position these close to the foam, forming an informal grouping (Fig. 2).

Now place the remaining six heads of golden rod and more spruce foliage (about eight short stems) in the centre of the arrangement.

The last flowers to be positioned are the 20 yellow carnations which should fill the whole shape. Be careful to radiate the flowers from a central point leaving them proud of the foliage and bauble background. Check that the material has covered all the foam, and use extra foliage if there are any gaps.

Finally prepare the ribbon bows as shown on page 16. At the top and bottom use a four-loop four-tail bow - at either side are two-loop two-tail bows.

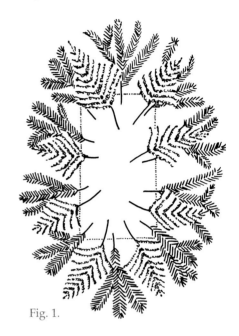

Fig. 1.

Fig. 2.

The fresh materials you will need

20 Yellow carnations
14 Heads of golden rod (solidago)
18 Stems of spruce foliage
 8 Gold baubles
 9 Branches of variegated holly
 8 Yards of golden ribbon

MANTLE MAGIC

Three separate arrangements are used on this mantlepiece to create a lush Christmas decoration containing plenty of different foliage which can easily be gathered during a countryside walk.

How it is made

Find three waterproof trays which will take blocks of Oasis and fit safely on the mantle you are decorating. Tape the well-soaked foam into the trays and place in their final position. For added safety put some Oasis fix under the trays to stick them to the mantle.

Use sprigs of blue spruce to create the offset triangular outline of the outside arrangements (Fig. 1) and amplify with holly . Use some ivy to provide outside trailing stems to break the base line. Try to build these two arrangements with the same material, at the same time, so that they develop mirror images. Cut the candles to three different heights and using candle holders position to follow the line of the triangle. Fill in the shape with holly and ivy foliage.

Determine the height of the centre arrangement with the figure, and then start to make a background of holly, ivy and spruce foliage in a fan shape (Fig. 2). Cut one of the red candles just shorter than the other two and position in front of the figure. Fill in the shape of the arrangement with foliage, berries and the flower heads of wild ivy.

The completing touch is to position the fresh red carnations. If youhave only a few flowers, simply strengthen the triangular shape of the two outside arrangements. If you have more, use them in the central arrangement as well.

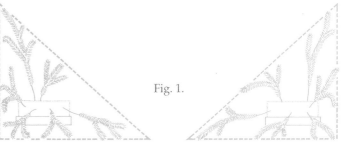

Fig. 1.

Fig. 2.

The fresh material you will need
9 Red carnations
9 Red candles
Blue spruce foliage
Holly foliage of various types
Ivy, some with flower heads

SCENTED BASKET

Roses, carnations and hyacinths fill this basket with colour and perfume. It could easily be repeated without the baubles, holly and snow flakes at any time of the winter.

How it is made

Line the basket with black polythene. Find a round deep dish and push in a block of Oasis wet foam. Place the dish on the right hand side of the basket.

Start the arrangement with holly and spruce foliage interspersed with September flowers to cover the right hand edge of the basket and to provide height at the back (Fig.1).

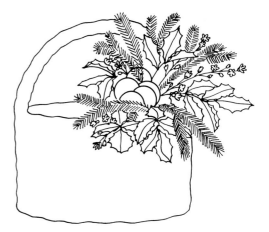

Fig. 1.

Fill in the centre with foliage and place the baubles at the front edge of the basket.

Define the outside edges of the arrangement with seven roses to give the sweeping circular shape (Fig.2). Use the remaining roses to fill out the informal shape of the arrangement, without covering the handle of the basket. By cutting the stems of the roses to different lengths you will automatically recess some of the blooms below the overall depth of flowers.

The carnations are used to fill in any gaps and to create a contrast of flower size. Complete the arrangement with the snow flake crystals distributed around the arrangement at different angles. Finally position the pots of hyacinths and ivy to the left of the arrrangement packing moist moss between the pots.

Fig. 2.

The material you will need
20 Pink roses
 6 Sprays of carnations
 3 Pots of pink hyacinths
 1 Pot of trailing ivy
10 Sprays of September flowers
 3 Sprays spruce foliage
 3 Sprays holly foliage
12 Snow crystals
 5 Pink baubles

DOOR GARLAND

Using a ready-made ring of evergreen foliage, this welcoming door decoration has been made into an individual arrangement using simple material and beautiful red and gold ribbons.

How it is made

Check the ring of evergreen foliage for a hanging loop. If missing, add one by pushing a wire through the ring and bending it back on itself (Fig. 1). This will give you the point of reference for the top of the arrangement.

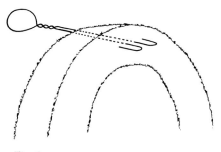

Fig. 1.

Begin by wiring all the material and making the ribbons. Wire the fir cones as shown on page 15 and give them a gentle spray of gold paint to add lustre. All wire stems should be long enough to go through the mossed ring and double back so that the items are secure.

Prepare the bundles of cinnamon sticks (Fig. 1) by wiring and covering the wire with ribbon. See page 19 for details.

Begin with the arrangement of material at the bottom of the ring. Group three cones to the left of centre and one to the right. Between them, position the bundle of cinnamon sticks with the ribbon attached. Around the edge use sprigs of holly foliage to act as a foil.

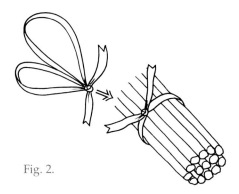

Fig. 2.

Now complete the groups of material at the sides of the ring. These are not completely symmetrical but are equally balanced. Position the groups of red berries in the blank green spaces of the ring and finally fix the six-loop ribbon bow at the top of the arrangement.

The material you will need
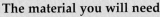
1 Ring of spruce foliage
3 Bundles of cinnamon sticks
9 Fir cones
5 Sprigs of holly foliage
8 Sprigs of red berries
3 Yards of narrow red ribbon
3 Yards of wide red ribbon

CANDLE RING

This cornucopia of fruits, nuts and berries is overflowing with rich colours and interesting textures. As a Christmas table centre it epitomises the celebration of sharing and plenty.

How it is made

This arrangement uses artificial material and you should therefore use foam for dried material in the standard ring. Push each candle into a holder and position the four white candles equally around the circle.

Start by going around the outside of the circle with various types of holly foliage, mixing sprigs of variegated holly with others of green with berries (Fig. 1). Use the peanuts around opposite candles to give you a starting point followed by groups of fir cones with foliage (Fig. 2).

At the other two candles use poinsettias, apples and baubles to cover the mechanics and create a tight group of overlapping material (Fig. 3).

Now fill in between the candles. At the four o'clock position is a group of five apples on a bed of holly. At the eight o'clock position are two bunches of blue spruce foliage with cones. At the ten o'clock position nine red baubles. At the one o'clock position more spruce foliage with nuts and cones.

Now that most of the circle is complete check for any gaps and if necessary fill with holly foliage and berries.

Fig. 1.

Fig. 2.

The material you will need
- 20 Artificial apples
- 24 Wired peanuts
- 24 Red poinsettia blooms
- 24 Sprigs of various types of holly
- 24 Red baubles
- 6 Sprigs of blue spruce
- 4 White candles

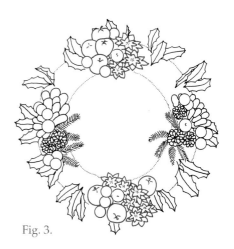

Fig. 3.

Mirror Garland

This sweeping garland in gold and pink uses different baubles, gilt toys and soft full ribbons to make a spectacular decoration around a mirror. Using ready-made artificial lengths of foliage allows preparations to be made well in advance of the festivities.

How it is made

For successful results this garland needs to be decorated when the greenery is in place on the wall. Start by fixing the greenery to the wall with small nails. Check that the curves match each other in width and depth.

Wire each of the baubles so that they hang easily on a ring at the end of the wire. Mix the various types along the length of the greenery making sure they match the curve of the background, but do not all follow a centre line (Fig. 1).

Wire each of the musical instruments and position these in the gaps between the baubles making sure that they are not all flat to the face of the garland. Make the six double-loop bows (see page 16) from 1" ribbon and position three on each side of the mirror.

Now make the two matching ribbons of eight-loops four-tails from the remainder of the 1" ribbon. Position these at the ends of the garland to hide the nails and to soften the effect. Create the ringlet tails by running the ribbon between your thumb and the back of the scissors or knife.

Finish with the central ribbon bow of ten-loops and four long tails, which is made from the 2" ribbon. Arrange the tails in attractive positions.

The material you will need

8 Golden baubles
12 Gilded baubles
8 Clear baubles with internal decorations
16 Gilt toys (trumpets, horns, etc)
26 Yards of 1" pink ribbon
7 Yards of 2" pink ribbon

Fig. 1.

CHRISTMAS CARNATIONS

The classic L-shape arrangement is ideal for a mantlepiece display. Variegated holly and red candles ensure a traditional feel and unusual lotus seed heads add a different texture.

How it is made

Use a narrow waterproof tray which will sit safely on the mantlepiece. Fix two foam anchors to the base and push on a block of Oasis foam, previously soaked in water.

Start the L-shape outline with the painted stems of birch twigs (Fig. 1).

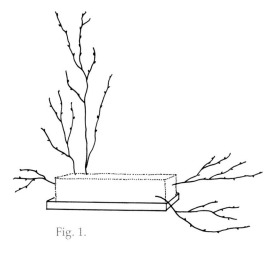

Fig. 1.

The candles are cut to different lengths and pushed directly into the wet foam. Use the holly as the major points of the triangle (Fig. 2) and the rest of the different foliage to cover the foam block and create the immediate shape.

Position the lotus seed heads deep within the foliage to add weight to the base line.

Now use the carnations to fill out the shape pointing them all in slightly different directions.

Finish off with a few strategically placed twigs of beech to ensure their red points are evenly situated around the triangular outline.

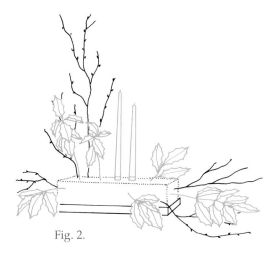

Fig. 2.

The material you will need
12 Red carnations
 3 Lotus seed heads
 7 Stems variegated holly foliage
 9 Stems Leylandii foliage
11 Pieces of spruce foliage
 8 Beech twigs painted red
 2 Red candles

GOLD & RED TREE

Decorating a Christmas tree is traditionally one of placing a lifetimes reminiscences on display. If you have the opportunity here is an organised design which can be used as a starting point.

How it is made

Start by making the ribbon bows which will form the overall theme of the tree decoration. (see page 16). Note the different uses for each ribbon - the red and gold is used with baubles - the tartan with some of the toy instruments - the gold lace with bunches of nuts.

Wire each bauble (Fig. 1), and then add a red and gold double-loop ribbon between the wires and over the bauble (Fig. 2). Twist the wire to secure the ribbon in position. Use a similar technique to add ribbon bows to the other material.

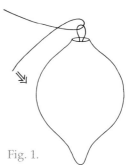

Fig. 1.

Check the tree lights for safety and fix in a spiral around the tree. Position the musical instruments evenly around the face of the tree, fixing some of them with tartan ribbons. Follow these with the round gold baubles with added ribbon bows. Now hang the droplet-shaped red baubles evenly around the tree.

The bunches of nuts and red balls are the last of the major items to be added, filling the gaps and balancing the red and gold elements.

Position the top-most ribbon of eight-loops and two long tails to provide a unifying summit.

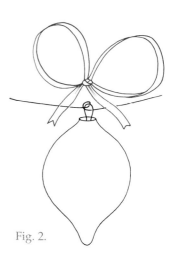

Fig. 2.

The material you will need
20 Gold round baubles
36 Gilt musical instruments
15 Droplet-shaped red baubles
10 Bunches of different nuts
10 Bunches of red balls
 8 Yards each of three different ribbons

If the tree is to be viewed all round, the rumber of items should be increased by 25%

GOLDEN CIRCLET

A wall decoration which uses the gilded circles of intertwined vine stems is ideal at Christmas time. The fresh foliage should enhance the base and not overwhelm the golden ring.

How it is made

Take a small piece of Oasis foam about three inches long, one inch wide and one inch deep. Soak well in water. Now use florist tape to secure this in position at the base of the ring (Fig. 1).

Start with dark green foliage around the edge of the oval shape. Keep the outline in proportion to the size of the ring - just a little wider and not too deep. Overlap the original layer with contrasting green foliage.

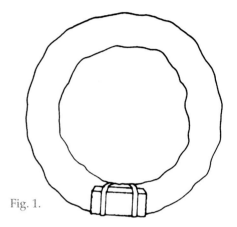

Now take the blue spruce foliage and fill in the centre of the arrangement. Wire the fir cone and position as the focal point directly above the ring base.

The ribbon bow is made in three sections. First make several loops of ribbon and pinch the ends together. Use a stub wire to tightly bind the ribbon ends together and to make a stem (Fig.2). Push this upwards into the foam just below the fir cone.

Now make two ribbon tails of different lengths. Cut a 'V' shape from one end of a length of ribbon and then use wire to make a double leg wire stem around the opposite end (Fig. 3). Position the ribbon tails separately.

Use the three lotus seed heads to finish off, two at the bottom right, just below the bow, and one at the top diagonally opposite.

Fig. 1.

Fig. 2.

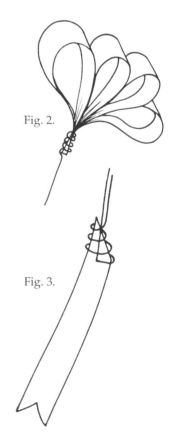

Fig. 3.

The fresh material you will need
    Pine foliage (Pinus)
    Blue spruce foliage (Picea)
    Fir foliage (Abies)
  3 Lotus seed heads
  1 Fir cone
    Red ribbon

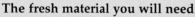

SILVER AND SNOW

This attractive ring of white and silver material is simply contrasted with small areas of holly foliage, red ribbons and sprigs of spruce. The beauty of the glass bubbles and white shells adds a fresh dimension to a standard idea.

How it is made

Buy a standard ring which contains foam for dried material. Cover all this foam with reindeer moss so that you will not have to worry too much about show-through of the foam.

Fit the silver candles into holders and position these accurately at four points of the compass. Check that the candles are vertical.

Around the base of each candle use foliage to create a contrast of colour. On the north and south candles use variegated holly with berries. On the other two use spruce foliage and multi-looped red ribbons (Fig. 1).

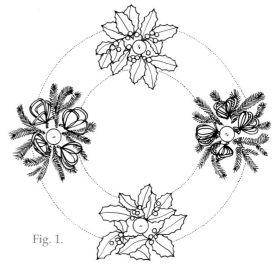

Fig. 1.

Use sea lavender to the left of each candle to create a linking element (Fig. 2). The gap between the south and west candle is filled with a large bunch of white Christmas roses and a host of glass bubbles. Between west and north are white sea shells and more Christmas roses. Between north and east use glass bubbles and silver poinsettia flowers. The gap between the east and south candles is filled with white sea shells and silver poinsettias.

When positioning the material for a table arrangement remember that the viewing angle will be low and the sides should be full.

Fig. 2.

The material you will need
- 12 White sea shells
- 24 White Christmas roses
- 24 Silver poinsettia flowers
- 6 Sprigs of spruce foliage with cones
- 2 Large bunches of glass bubbles
- 1 Large bunch of sea lavender
- 4 Yards of slender red ribbon
  Reindeer moss
- 4 Silver candles

SANTA'S ROSE DISPLAY

The focal point of this arrangement is not the red roses contrasted with white gypsophila and delicate grey foliage but the simple Santa Claus figure which is placed strategically.

How it is made

Soak a round of green Oasis foam and push onto the stand, securing with tape. Fit the white candle into a holder and push this centrally into the foam.

Start the arrangement with five pieces of eucalyptus and five pieces of spruce foliage around the edge of the circle (Fig. 1). Create height in the centre by positioning the remaining eucalyptus and spruce foliage close to the candle (Fig. 2).

Wire the Santa figure and position as the focal point at the base of the candle.

Prepare the five red bells into a cascade using red ribbon (see page 18 for details). Place to the left of the figure, ensuring that the bottom of the cascade hangs below the level of the flowers.

Create a dome-shape with the viburnum and santolina foliage interspersed with sprigs of gypsophila flowers. Now use the roses to surround the figure.

Check that all the foam is hidden by the material and use the remaining sprigs to fill any gaps.

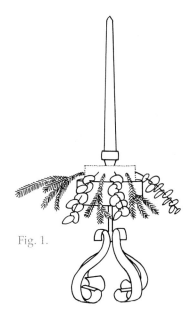

Fig. 1.

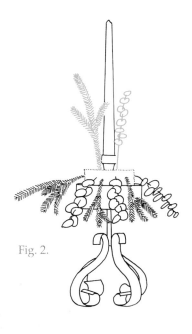

Fig. 2.

The fresh material you will need

10 Red roses
 5 Red bells
 5 Sprigs santolina foliage
 9 Sprigs spruce foliage
 7 Sprigs gypsophila flowers
 9 Sprigs eucalyptus foliage
 7 Sprigs viburnum foliage with buds
 1 White candle

CONES AND CANDLES

The contrast of a group of pure white candles against the dark textured beauty of three types of cones and three different sorts of evergreen foliage provides an impressive combination.

How it is made

For a long-lasting arrangement use green wet foam as the base to hold the fresh material. The evergreen foliage may not take up a lot of water but it allows you the option of misting regularly over the leaves with plain water.

Fix two foam anchors into the bottom of the bowl and push on a block of foam previously soaked in water.

Start by defining the height with a piece of branching yew and then the two base points of the triangle with blue cedar branches (Fig. 1).

Fig. 1.

The five white pencil candles are pushed directly into the Oasis at different depths to create a gentle spiral shape.

Use some evergreen foliage around the edge of the bowl to hide the mechanics and soften the hard edge. Wire each of the cones separately and use as shown in Fig. 2. For step-by-step instructions on wiring cones see page 15.

The artichoke heads usually have a stem but if this is not long enough add a double leg wire so that they can be placed in position on the right-hand side.

Finish off with foliage to fill in the outline and hide the stems of material and the base of the candles.

Fig. 2.

The material you will need
2   Artichoke heads
1   Piece of yew foliage (Taxus)
5   Pieces of blue cedar (Cedrus)
5   Pieces pine foliage (Pinus)
3   Cones of blue cedar
5   Ribbon cones
2   Pine cones
5   Thin white candles.

DECORATED BRANCHES

Quick and easy, this decoration works well in a formal surrounding. You could add further material including sweets, ribbons and other tree decorations for a fuller effect.

How it is made

Half fill the jug with water and push a piece of chicken wire into the neck to give some support to the twigs and flower stems.

First position the three white twigs at the back of the jug in an attractive way. These instructions are necessarily vague as no two twigs are the same, but use the tallest in the centre and the one which bends most on the left hand side.

Now fill the front of the jug with the pot containing the spider plant (*Tradescantia*) which should, for preference, have several trailing stems carrying miniature plants at the end of each one (Fig. 1). Make sure the rim of the pot is not obvious. If necessary repot the plant into a white pot.

Now tie the nine baubles to the twigs using fine red ribbons. Use enough ribbon so that a four loop bow can be created with decent sized tails.

Use the 3 stems of dark green ruscus foliage and then the 3 stems of September flowers to fill in the background and to act as a contrasting foil between the white jug and the white twigs.

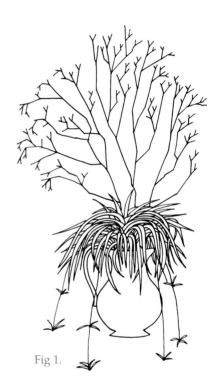

Fig 1.

The material you will need
9 Glass baubles
3 Twigs painted white
1 Spider plant (*Tradescantia*)
3 Stems of ruscus foliage
3 Stems of September flowers

WELCOME WREATH

More like a star burst than a circular wreath, this traditional front door decoration is jammed with different material and topped by a professional-looking bow.

How it is made

Buy a plastic circular wreath base which is already fitted with Oasis fresh foam. Soak well in water and position flat on a table. If there is no hook then use strong wire to create the necessary hanging position before you add any material.

Start by using pieces of spruce foliage evenly spaced around the outside of the wheel to create the radiating outline (Fig.1). See that this foliage reaches the level of the table.

Fig. 1.

Now use the variegated holly and blue spruce and pine foliage to cover the ring. Make sure there is enough variegated holly foliage to feature all round the circle for this adds lightness to the wreath.

Add a wire stem to each fir cone (Fig. 2) and twist three stems together to make a tight bunch. Include these at different angles around the wreath.

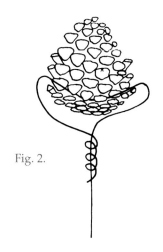

Fig. 2.

Fill in the centre with foliage as necessary. Finally push the red berries into position and top off with the six loop bow. See page 16 for step-by-step instructions. Arrange the ribbon tails attractively.

The fresh material you will need
Spruce foliage
Variegated holly foliage
Blue spruce foliage
Pine foliage
Larch cones
Spruce cones
Ribbon bow with wire edges

LUXURY CHOCOLATE BOX

Decorating presents is a dying art, but this idea shows how a few pieces of ribbon and some gilded seed heads can transform an ordinary box into something very special and individual.

How it is made

Begin by decorating the poppy heads and the fir cone. The pepper pot ends of the poppy heads are covered with glue and, while this is wet, dipped into gold glitter. Use a fine brush to paint the ends of the cone scales with gold paint. Leave the poppy heads and the cone to dry thoroughly before continuing, preferably overnight.

Fig. 1.

Start the arrangement by taking the widest ribbon and folding it as shown in Fig. 1. Staple the folds together and then stick in position with glue.

Stick down the three cinnamon sticks and the three poppy heads using the minimum amount of clear glue. Glue the cone in the centre to cover the staple used on the wide ribbon.

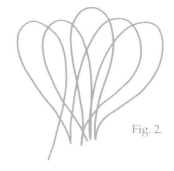

Fig. 2.

Make the wire loop bow with several small loops of the material held together with clear tape (Fig.2). Stick this on the chocolate box with glue.

The last bow is the lace ribbon which is stapled together and then glued to hide any of the mechanics.

The material you will need
- 3 Poppy heads
- 3 Cinnamon sticks
- 1 Fir cone
- 4 Types of ribbon

WHITE LILIES & CANDLES

The beauty of large white lilies and simple white candles is contrasted here with dark foliage and seed heads. The end result is a stunning arrangement with a calm religious feel.

How it is made

Fix two foam anchors to the base of the bowl and push two blocks of wet oasis firmly onto the spikes. Cut the blocks so that you create the necessary steps for the different height of the candles. Prepare the candles with toothpicks (see page 18) and place into position. Cover the top of the foam around the candles with reindeer moss.

Use five pieces of spruce foliage to create the outline shape of the arrangement (Fig. 1). Use six pieces of variegated holly to fill in around this shape. Now place the twisting hazel twigs around the outside to break the triangular outline (Fig. 2).

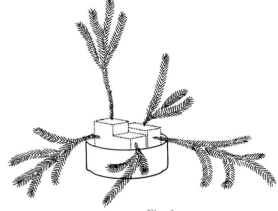

Fig. 1.

Wire the fir cones separately and position these in two groups of five - one just below the right hand candle and the other on the left hand side. Use three lotus seed heads to link these two bunches of cones together.

The positioning of the lilies is important. See that there are buds at the top of the arrangement and that the open flowers are used in the centre to draw the eye to the focal point of the three plain candles.

Finally use some spruce foliage and hazel twigs to break any flat or bare areas.

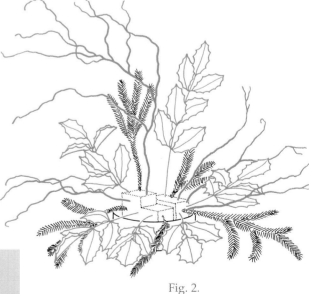

Fig. 2.

The material you will need
5	Stems of white lilies
8	Sprigs of variegated holly
6	Pieces of spruce foliage
5	Pieces of hazel twigs
10	Fir cones
3	Lotus seed heads
	Reindeer moss
3	White candles

CARNATIONS AND CANDLES

Rich red carnations contrast well with dainty September flowers and fresh evergreen foliage. Because it is relatively small this arrangement can be quickly copied on a limited budget.

How it is made

Fit an anchor to the base of the vase with Oasis Fix and push a round of wet Oasis onto the spikes.

Prepare the candle as shown on page 18 with toothpicks and position centrally on the foam. To hide the mechanics cover the foam with reindeer moss, especially around the candle.

Go around the edge of the vase with sprigs of different foliage, mixing blue spruce with holly and mistletoe (Fig. 1). Also at this level use three carnations, three sprigs of September flowers and three fir cones (Fig. 2).

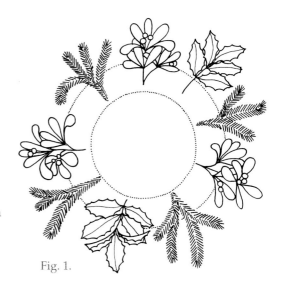

Fig. 1.

Now work up the height of the arrangement to create a dome shape, mixing the different materials as you go. Make sure the September flowers are proud of the overall outline so they are not lost between the foliage.

Position the two bunches of red berries on opposite sides of the arrangement to provide interesting highlights.

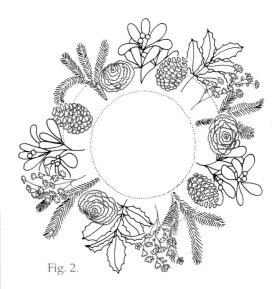

Fig. 2.

The fresh material you will need
- 10 Red carnations
- 6 Sprigs of holly
- 6 Sprigs of blue spruce
- 6 Sprigs of mistletoe
- 6 Fir cones
- 10 Small bunches of September flowers
- 2 Bunches of red berries
- Reindeer moss
- 1 Red candle

NUTS & WINTER FOLIAGE

This arrangement uses all artificial material, so can be brought out year after year. The grouping of material shown here is highly fashionable, and is easy to copy.

How it is made

Fit two anchors to the base of the bowl and push on blocks of Dry Foam to fill the whole bowl. Tape toothpicks to the candle and position centrally on the foam.

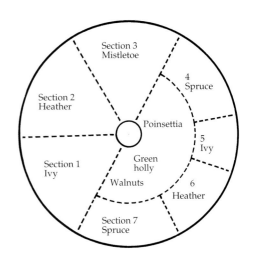

The plan view of the arrangement shows it is basically split into segments. Start by overlaying six stems of ivy to make the largest section 1.

To the left of that is twelve small bunches of dark green heather, followed by twelve sprigs of mistletoe (sections 2 and 3). The next four sections are not filled up as far as the candle, but leave space for other material.

In the topmost part of sections 4 and 5 place three poinsettia heads close together to form a mass of red. In the blank area above sections 6 and 7 use six heads of holly with berries and top this off with seven gilded walnuts.

Use five more gilded walnuts to add extra sparkle to the mistletoe foliage.

To provide an intesting texture to the dark green foliage of section 2, wire thirteen chestnuts as shown on page 15 and position in a group.

Top view

To complete the arrangement take eight bunches of berried stems and position as shown

The artificial material you will need
- 3 Red poinsettia heads
- 12 Gilded walnuts
- 13 Chestnuts
- 6 Sprigs of berried holly
- 8 Bunches of berried stems
- 9 Stems of variegated ivy
- 12 Stems of mistletoe
- 17 Small bunches of heather foliage
- 5 Sprigs of spruce foliage
- 1 White candle

WHITE CHRISTMAS

Ideal for Christmas, Hogmanay or Burns Night this pure white arrangement relies on a strong colour for the ribbon bow and deep red candles.

How it is made

Fix a foam anchor into the metal base with Oasis Fix. Push a round of wet foam onto the anchor after soaking in water.

Cut one of the candles slightly shorter than the other and push them both directly into the wet foam. Ensure they are vertical and then place the multi-loop ribbon bow centrally.

Use three pieces of ivy and three pieces of conifer foliage to make the trailing base points (Fig. 1). Then position pieces of blue conifer foliage to form the background and start the outline.

Six of the freesias are placed around the edges to define the crescent shape (Fig. 2).

Now fill in the centre with sprays of white chrysanthemums mixed with foliage and freesias. Try to position the freesias so that they face in different directions. This will show the overall form of this beautiful flower. Make sure that there is space around the candles to allow them to be burnt without danger.

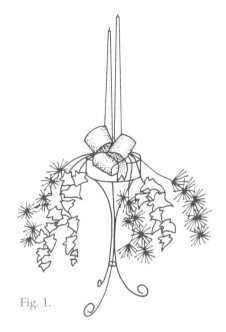

Fig. 1.

Fig. 2.

The material you will need

18 White freesias
4 Sprays white chrysanthemums
3 Stems trailing variegated ivy
8 Pieces blue cedar foliage
3 Long stems pine foliage
2 Candles
1 Ribbon bow

83

FRUITS AND BERRIES

A simple candle decoration is made excitingly different with various fruits and berries. This all-round display is full of colour and textures, and would make an excellent table centre.

How it is made

Fill the white bowl with foam for dried material. Use a knife to cut the foam creating a flat topped cone.

Tape toothpicks to the base of the candle and push gently into the foam at the dead centre of the bowl. Surround the base of the candle with holly foliage so that the foam is hidden (Fig. 1).

Fig. 1.

Now start to group the material around the sides. A bed of holly foliage on the right hand side is probably the best place to start. Make sure you overlap the edge of the bowl. Top this off with the four pomegranate fruits, a few Christmas roses and some gilded mistletoe (Fig. 2).

Now move to the left and position the group of brown seed heads, once again overlapping the edge of the bowl. The next group round consists of red holly berries that have been gently frosted to add a new texture. Follow this with spruce foliage and five Christmas roses.

Fig. 2.

Towards the back of the arrangement there is a group of five pears mixed with mistletoe foliage followed by more holly leaves topped off with a large group of brazil nuts.

The material you will need
- 7 Christmas roses
- 4 Pomegranates
- 12 Sprigs gilded mistletoe
- 20 Sprigs variegated holly with berries
- 5 Artificial pears
- 5 Sprigs red berries
- 12 Wired brazil nuts
- 9 Bunches of seed heads
- Spruce foliage
- 1 Red candle

ROSE TABLE CENTRE

The ideal shape and colouring for a winter dinner party. The flowers are kept low enough to allow easy conversation and the white candles will add a sparkle to the silver and glasses.

How it is made

The base is a simple waterproof tray with low edges. Fix two foam anchors to the base with Oasis Fix. Push a block of Oasis previously soaked onto the anchors.

Start by going around the edges with the foliage making a long oval (Fig. 1). Now follow the same shape, alternating roses with carnations (Fig. 2).

Place the three candles into position in a straight line down the centre of the oval. Push the outside two just a littler further down into the foam to give a variation of height.

Cover the foam with short pieces of holly and evergreen foliage. Make sure that the spaces between the candles are covered.

Now build up the flowering outline keeping the carnations just slightly recessed below the level of the beautiful roses which should dominate.

Fig. 1.

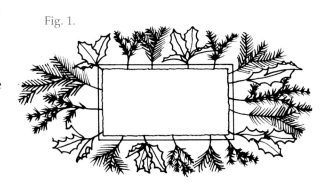

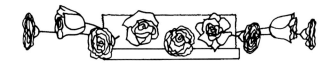

Fig. 2.

The fresh material you will need
24 Red roses
24 Yellow carnations
    Holly foliage
    Yew foliage
 3 White candles

PAINTER'S PALETTE

A simple arrangement dominated by the pink Painter's Palette (Anthurium) which should last a long time in the home. It would be quick to make at any time in the winter months.

How it is made

Fill the jug with water to within three inches of the lip.

Start by finding holly foliage which will overlap the edges of the jug and use at least two pieces pointing downwards. These pieces will ensure the jug is visually linked with the flowers and becomes a visual part of the arrangement.

Now create the overall dimensions using holly and eucalyptus foliage mixed together (Fig. 1). The height should be no more than one and a half times taller than the jug. The overall width should be approximately the same as the overall height of jug and foliage.

Fig. 1.

Place the three anthurium heads within this foliage shape, defining the face of the arrangement (Fig. 2).

Now position the five lily stems, ensuring there is a good presence of white flowers between the anthuriums and some blooms protrude outside the mass of foliage.

Finish the arrangement with the September flowers breaking the outline of the arrangement.

The material you will need
 5 Lily stems with white flowers
 3 Anthurium heads, preferably pink
 7 Stems of variegated holly foliage
 7 Stems of eucalyptus foliage
10 Stems of September flowers

Fig. 2.

TARTAN CIRCLE

Just seven white chrysanthemums hold this Yuletide arrangement together as an entity. Once again the variety of different foliage colours and textures is important to add variety.

How it is made

Buy a circular Oasis holder 12 inches in diameter. Thoroughly soak the foam in water before you start. Push the candles into the foam evenly around the circle, making sure they are vertical (Fig. 1).

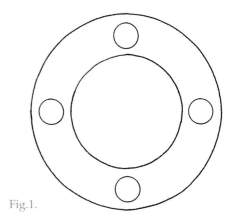

Fig.1.

Cut the evergreen foliage in short pieces and go around the edge of the circle mixing blue spruce with juniper and variegated holly (Fig. 2). Use pieces of hebe and other foliage to cover the surface of the foam, seeing that the inside is also covered.

Now place the seven white chrysanthemums around the circle. Ensure that they are pointing in different directions.

Wire loops of tartan ribbon as shown on page 16 and push into position at four points between each candle.

Finish off with the seed heads. Make four bunches of poppy heads by wiring three per bunch and place around the circle. Then wire two bunches of walnuts, three per bunch, before positioning towards the centre of the arrangement. Finally use the lotus heads and red holly berries to add extra colour.

Fig. 2.

The material you will need
- 7 White chrysanthemums
- 12 Poppy seed heads
- 5 Lotus seed heads
- 6 Walnuts
  Holly foliage
  Blue spruce foliage
  Juniper foliage
  Variegated hebe foliage
- 4 Red candles
  Tartan ribbon

WOODLAND WONDER

This low table decoration is beautifully simple and retains a good contrast between the formal white lilies and the rustic foliage and cones. The white bowl is well hidden to give an informal elongated mound effect.

How it is made

Fix a foam anchor to the inside of the bowl and push on wet Oasis so that the foam is proud of the rim by about 3cm (1 inch). Cut the candles to different lengths and push these as a group into the centre of the foam. Cover the surface with reindeer moss.

Fig. 1.

Use six pieces of variegated holly to define the outside perameters of the arrangement (Fig. 1). Use four more pieces of holly to hide the base of the candles.

Between the holly, place pieces of spruce foliage (Fig. 2) making sure these overlap the edge of the bowl, almost down to the table. Now break the outline with stems of ivy ensuring some point out above the mound and others trail onto the table.

On each side of the arrangement are two cones which should be positioned beside each other but at different heights.

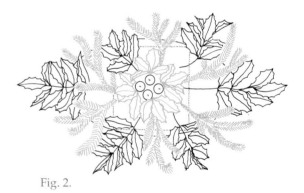

Fig. 2.

Now use the lilies around the arrangement at different heights and pointing out from the centre. These flowers should be positioned so that they are growing directly out of the foliage - no stems should be obvious.

Finally fill in any gaps with straw moss.

The fresh material you will need
10 White lilies
10 Sprigs of variegated holly
 6 Sprigs of spruce foliage
 6 Ivy stems
 4 Cones
   Reindeer moss, straw moss
 4 White candles

RUSTIC DRESSER

This long-lasting collection of artificial materials is sufficiently varied to provide an arrangement which will grace any home for many years. The loose style however does have a balance - material featured prominently on one side is used subtly on the other.

How it is made

Use a block of foam for dried flowers and position in the ceramic basket so that there is at least 3 cm (1 inch) proud of the rim.

Start by defining the width and height of the arrangement with five stems carrying small gold cones (Fig. 1). Some of the fir foliage is used to complete this low triangular shape, using short stems along the base line to hide the edge of the ceramic basket.

Complete the outside of the arrangement with stems of variegated holly and a good bunch of mistletoe at the top (Fig. 2). Now use the golden acorns and red berried material to mirror each other. There are three stems of red berries and one spray of acorns pointing upwards and left, while one spray of red berries and three bunches of acorns are placed pointing downwards on the right hand side (Fig. 3).

Now complete the central mass of colour. Run an S-shaped line of variegated holly through the centre, with white Christmas roses running on either side. The white berries are used heavily to the right side, but with only a few used on the left. Use the small poinsettia flowers on the left mixed in with variegated holly.

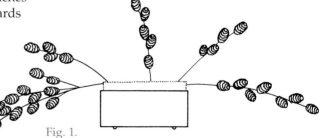

Fig. 1.

Finish the arrangement with a few extra sprigs of mistletoe and fir foliage to link all the elements together.

The artificial material you will need

12	Christmas roses
15	Small poinsettias
5	Stems of red berries
6	Stems of variegated holly
5	Bunches of golden acorns
5	Stems of mistletoe
7	Stems of golden cones
5	Stems of fir foliage
5	Stems of white berries

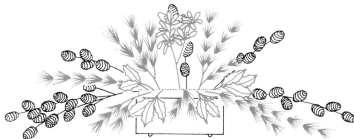

Fig. 2.

Fig. 3.

INDEX

*Oasis is the trade mark of Smithers Oasis

the immigration into South Wales from far and wide during the boom years.

The hectic activity in Cardiff as it grew to become one of the world's busiest ports created a prosperous city in which civic pride could be given full expression. This is nowhere more evident than in Cardiff's white-stoned neoclassical Civic Centre, an outstanding example of its kind. As the city matured in the twentieth century, its architectural ex___ was enhanced by large area___ parklands and gardens.

Cardiff was declared capi___ Wales in 1955, making it Europe's youngest capital city. In recent years its dynamic, restless reputation has been revived as imaginative plans for the development of Cardiff Bay – a vast enterprise which will reunite the city with its historic waterfront – begin to unfold.

with its wide, tree-lined avenues, immaculate parklands and fine municipal and government buildings, has a spacious, stately air.

History

Cardiff has a chequered past. From an important military base in Roman and medieval times, it declined into an insignificant coastal village in the eighteenth century only to be reborn in the last 200 years as a thriving coal-exporting port and capital city of Wales.

Its location, at the mouth of the River Taff, has always played a crucial role in its development. The Romans were the first to recognise Cardiff's

BELOW RIGHT Cardiff Castle began life as a Roman fort. Roman remains include a large section of the perimeter wall, distinguished from later work by a band of red stone.

BELOW Cardiff's medieval castle is shown here in an eighteenth-century print. The Cardiff which grew up around it in medieval times was a place of trade and barter, and by the fourteenth century had become a well-known Welsh port.

SITE OF THE
EAST GATE

PART OF THE NORMAN DEFENCES OF THE TOWN.
THROUGH THIS GATE CAME ALL WHO TRAVELLED THE
ANCIENT ROAD BETWEEN GLOUCESTER AND SWANSEA.
KNOWN AS PORTH CROCKERTON, FROM THE DISTRICT
OF CROCKHERBTOWN, POSSIBLY NAMED FOR THE FINE
VEGETABLE GARDENS OF THE 13TH CENTURY HOUSE
OF THE GREYFRIARS, CLOSE BY.
THE TOWN HOSPICE STOOD OUTSIDE THIS GATE.
RESTORED AFTER THE WELSH UPRISING OF 1404
THE FORTIFIED TRIPLE ARCHED STONE GATEWAY,
WITH SENTRY AND SLOPE HOUSES, WAS
DEMOLISHED IN 1781 TO IMPROVE THE TOLL ROAD.
IN THE 18TH CENTURY WITH THE BUILDING OF
THE GLAMORGANSHIRE CANAL,
CROCKHERBTOWN LOCK STOOD BY THE
SITE OF THE OLD GATE.
AT THE TURN OF THE CENTURY
THIS PLACE WAS STILL KNOWN AS
"THE PILLARS".
6
DONATED BY B.H.S.LTD, OCTOBER 1977

ABOVE Cardiff's numerous blue plaques tell visitors about the history of the city. This one, at the junction of The Friary and Queen Street, marks the site of the city's Norman east gate, demolished in 1781.

strategic value as a natural road junction with access to the sea. Their eight-acre (3 ha) fort, dating from AD 75, stood beside the river where the military road from their major

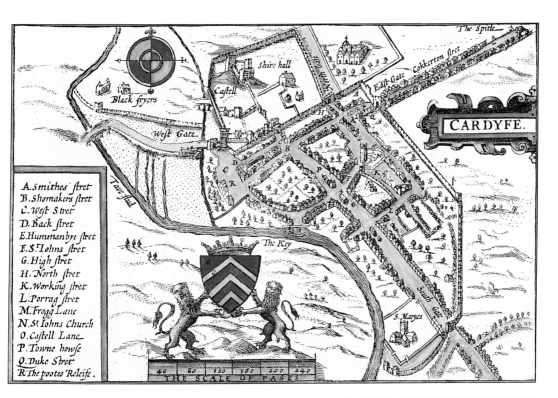

A.Smithes ſtret
B.Shomakers ſtret
C.Weſt S tret
D.Back ſtret
E.Hummanbye ſtret
F.St Iohns ſtret
G.High ſtret
H.North ſtret
K.Working ſtret
L.Porrag ſtret
M.Frogg Lane
N.St Iohns Church
O.Caſtell Lane
P.Towne howſe
Q.Duke Stret
R.The pootes Releiſe.

ABOVE John Speed's map of Cardiff in 1610 shows the town wall extending southwards from the castle to enclose a surprisingly small area. The course of the River Taff has since altered considerably and the last remains of the wall disappeared in the nineteenth century.

base at nearby Isca (Caerleon) to west Wales crossed the tidal estuary. As well as being the first settlers, the Romans may have given Cardiff its name – after the general Aulus Didius, Caer Didi referring to 'the fort of Didius'.

One thousand years later the invading Normans endorsed the Romans' strategic choice by using the crumbling ruins of the fort as the basis for their stronghold. By the thirteenth century a medieval township had grown up around the castle. Cardiff had begun to establish itself as a trading centre and Welsh port of some importance, for in 1581 it received its first royal charter, granted by Elizabeth I. But this recognition did nothing to create an

orderly civic life, for Elizabethan Cardiff was a town of 'rioters, cut-throats and pirates who infested the Bristol Channel'.

The town seemed doomed to decline. By the eighteenth century a shrinking population of only 1,500 lived here, quite unaware of the revolution which would shortly transform their sleepy backwater into one of the world's busiest ports.

ABOVE Late-eighteenth-century Cardiff, as can be seen from this artist's impression of 1797 by Thomas Rowlandson, was an ordinary country town. Soon the coal trade would change everything.

The Industrial Revolution arrived with whirlwind force in South Wales. In the teeming valleys to the north of Cardiff blast furnaces were fired up and countless coalmines were sunk. A canal link was completed between Cardiff and the valley communities in 1794, enabling iron and later coal to be transported quickly and cheaply to the coast. Cardiff's transformation was about to begin.

In 1839 the family which was to play the leading role in Cardiff's future development began its spectacularly successful entrepreneurial career when the second Marquess of Bute, the 'creator of modern Cardiff', opened his first dock. Railway links arrived between 1845 and 1850, by which time nearly three-quarters of a million tons of coal were being exported annually from

John Patrick Crichton-Stuart, the third Marquess of Bute, whose family were the creators of modern Cardiff. His immense wealth went into the rebuilding of Cardiff Castle. The foundations for the family's fortunes were laid by the second marquess, a man of great business acumen who founded the docks. His investment of £350,000 – his entire fortune – in the construction of the first of the Bute Docks earned the family a fabulous return as Cardiff grew to become one of the world's major coal-exporting ports.

ABOVE **In the late nineteenth and early twentieth centuries Cardiff's focal point was the booming docklands of Butetown, a mile or so south of the city centre. The railways brought coal from the South Wales valleys for shipment, a trade which peaked in 1913 when 10½ million tons of the 'black diamond' passed through the docks.**

RIGHT **The imposing Coal Exchange was the dockland nerve centre of Cardiff's coal business.**

the burgeoning port of Butetown. In 1861 this figure had grown to two million tons and in record-breaking 1913 Cardiff's 10½ million tons made it the world's premier coal-exporting port.

The population was also growing in quantum leaps. By 1850 it had increased to 30,000, by 1911 it stood at 182,000 and in 1931 it had risen to 227,000.

With the decline in the coal trade after the First World War, Cardiff gradually assumed a new white-collar role. Docks closed and offices opened; heavy industry was replaced by the machinery of government, commerce and administration. Cardiff was officially made a city in 1905 by Edward VII, and in 1955 became the Welsh capital.

Despite its status, Cardiff is not a typically Welsh place. Its colourful past has given it a hybrid, cosmopolitan character, and although Welsh-speaking intelligentsia increasingly make their presence felt in establishment circles, Cardiff is overwhelmingly English speaking – and in a unique way, for the vowel-stretching Cardiffian accent is as distinctive as anything spoken by a Cockney or Liverpudlian.

The city is the kingpin of south-east Wales, a region within which is concentrated most of the country's industry and commerce, not to mention three-quarters of the 2¾ million inhabitants. Nearly 300,000 people live in Cardiff itself, and around two million within an hour's drive of the capital.

According to the economic gurus, Cardiff can look forward to the twenty-first century with confidence. Not only is it poised to benefit further from its excellent communications with the rest of Britain, but the city is also renewing its links with the sea through an ambitious development programme to transform the old docklands.

ABOVE **This detail on the Victorian Pierhead Building in Cardiff's docklands symbolises the links between the Welsh valleys and Cardiff. The building is now witnessing a new chapter in the story of the waterfront as the Cardiff Bay redevelopment takes shape.**

BELOW **The splendid neoclassical architecture of the Civic Centre reaches its zenith at the City Hall.**

Cardiff Castle

ABOVE **The Animal Wall running along Castle Street is an apt introduction to Cardiff Castle's sense of light-hearted whimsy. Animals peering over the wall include an ant-eater, a sea-lion, a racoon and a vulture.**

Cardiff's city-centre castle is an outstanding three-dimensional site, historically as well as visually. First, there is the 2,000-year-old Roman fort which forms its foundations. Then there is the medieval stronghold built by the invading Normans. Last, but by no means least, is the nineteenth-century mansion, an extravagant fantasy palace which perfectly captures the jubilant spirit of the Victorian age.

These three historic strands are woven together within one large site. The castle's extensive Roman walls, ten feet (3 m) thick, owe their remarkable state of preservation to the earthen banks which hid them from view until excavation in the nineteenth century. Within the grounds stands the Norman keep, also exceptionally well preserved, crowning a steep mound ringed by a moat.

The castle as we see it today began to take shape in the thirteenth century, when it was strengthened to ward off the ever-present threat of attack. Like many other fortresses it fell into ruin after the Civil War of the seventeenth century; it was rescued from oblivion by the first Marquess of Bute in the late 1700s.

Its true saviour, though, was the third marquess, aided by architect

ABOVE **The walls of Cardiff Castle enclose a large area of grassland which gives some indication of the size and importance of the Roman fort which originally occupied this site.**

RIGHT **The castle's authentic medieval core still stands, enclosed within the extensive walls. The Norman stronghold, originally a timber stockade, was rebuilt in stone in the twelfth century.**

LEFT **Cardiff Castle is flanked by greenery, for although in the busy heart of the city it stands next to the open spaces of Bute Park. Park and castle were given to the city by the Bute family in 1947.**

ABOVE **The magnificent Clock Tower, built between 1869 and 1873 for the young, single third Marquess of Bute, was the ultimate bachelor apartment, with elaborate summer and winter smoking rooms and a bachelor bedroom complete with Roman bath. Whether or not the marquess ever enjoyed this retreat is open to debate, for he married in 1872.**

William Burges. The former was scholarly, shy and immensely wealthy, the latter extrovert, worldly and an unorthodox genius. They were the perfect match, a partnership – and firm friendship – which was to endure for sixteen years.

By the mid nineteenth century the Butes, owners of Cardiff's booming docklands, were fabulously rich. The third marquess, one of the world's wealthiest men with an annual income of £300,000, lavished much of his fortune on the wholesale reconstruction of the castle.

'Billy' Burges began remodelling the mansion-cum-castle in 1868. The end product has been described in many terms, ranging from brilliant to bogus, outrageous to opulent. To the purist the castle may seem nothing more than an over-the-top sham of gigantic proportions. But for most visitors this romantic palace is enchanting and entertaining, the perfect expression of Victorian self-confidence, energy and prosperity.

William Burges, the 'eccentric genius' who remodelled – not to say reinvented – Cardiff Castle, had a soaring Victorian vision which acknowledged few boundaries – due, some cynics suggest, to his short-sightedness and acquaintance with the opium pipe. He absorbed influences from the Middle Ages, the Renaissance and Islam to create a style of architecture which became known as Burgesian Gothic. The Marquess of Bute, Burges's ideal patron, allowed this extravagant architect full rein in his work at Cardiff.

The joint creators of the castle's lavish apartments and public rooms cast their net far and wide for inspiration, drawing on everything from medieval England to Arabia, from the Old Testament to the fairytales of Hans Christian Anderson. The rooms are laden with motifs, decoration and architectural features which reflect many different themes.

The attention to detail is everywhere quite overwhelming. The marquess's main bathroom, for example, is lined with sixty different types of marble. The Fairytale Nursery is decorated with a frieze of hand-painted tiles based on stories from *The Arabian Nights*, the Brothers Grimm and Hans Christian Anderson. The Summer Smoking Room contains a bronze model of the world inlaid into a tiled floor and a large chandelier representing the sun, all guarded by a chained dragon!

RIGHT The grand fireplace in the Banqueting Hall has an inscription and medieval decoration alluding to a twelfth-century episode in the castle's history when it was under the control of 'Robert the Consul', Earl of Gloucester.

RIGHT The Herbert Tower, remodelled between 1876 and 1889, contains the Arab Room, perhaps the most stunning in the entire castle. It is a shrine to Islamic influence, with studded marble walls lined with cedarwood rising to this astonishing gilded ceiling of rare complexity. The room is said to have been one of the Marquess of Bute's favourites.

LEFT **The fabulous Winter Smoking Room, part of a suite of rooms in the Clock Tower. Architect William Burges, applying 'the passing of time' as a central theme for the tower, made sure that the Marquess of Bute was also supplied with a Summer Smoking Room!**

BELOW **Work began on the opulently decorated Bute Tower in 1873. Its astonishingly eclectic series of rooms is crowned by a tiled and fountained roof garden, intended to bring the atmosphere of medieval Provence to Cardiff.**

It is said that the marquess's favourite room was the Arab Room, so it is fitting that it has a plaque commemorating his partnership with Burges, who died in 1881. Its matter-of-fact message, at complete odds with their flamboyant creation, simply reads, 'John Marquess of Bute built this 1881. William Burges designed it.'

Not content with Cardiff Castle alone, the marquess also commissioned Burges to build him a country retreat. The ensuing creation of Castell Coch, perched on a wooded cliff just a few miles north of the city at Tongwynlais, is pure fairytale, straight out of the pages of *The Sleeping Beauty*.

Cardiff Castle is the home of two military museums dedicated to the Welch Regiment and the First the Queen's Dragoon Guards.

The Civic Centre

The Bute family continued to influence the development of Cardiff when they sold Cathays Park to Cardiff Corporation in 1898. The site, close to the castle and main shopping streets, was earmarked for municipal development – not the usual group of undistinguished council offices, but a collection of buildings with near-imperial overtones harmoniously arranged in a rectangular plan with wide, tree-lined avenues and beautiful parklands.

Cardiff's Civic Centre never fails to impress visitors to the city. Its neoclassical white-stoned edifices, regarded as a world-ranking example of civic architecture, have drawn comparisons with Washington DC and New Delhi. Their sense of unity and delicate balance of architectural

LEFT From its perch on the dome of the City Hall, this fearsome representation of the Welsh dragon – Wales's national symbol – looks out over Cardiff.

RIGHT The City Hall's richly decorative 194-foot (59 m) clock tower displays the skills of the stonecarver to good effect.

detail with sculpture reflect a mixture of unbridled flair and careful planning.

The domed City Hall of 1906, home of Cardiff City Council, was designed by architects Lanchester, Stewart and Rickards. As impressive internally as it is from the outside, it contains the Marble Hall with monolithic columns of Sienna marble and 'Heroes of Wales' statues.

It is flanked by the National Museum of Wales of 1927 and the Law Courts of 1906, an imposing trio of buildings at the front of the Civic Centre which almost eclipses the architectural riches which lie behind. On the western side stands Mid Glamorgan County Hall (1912) with its striking portico of Corinthian columns. Next in line is the University of Cardiff's Bute Building (1916), a more subdued interpretation of the neoclassical style, which diminishes even further in the simple lines of the Temple of Peace and Health (1938) next door.

The core of the Civic Centre is devoted to the delightful Alexandra Gardens, whose eastern side is faced by the long, ornamental façade of Cardiff University (1909). The northern end of the Civic Centre is the home of the Welsh Office (1938) and the Crown Offices (1980), the centre for government administration in Wales.

TOP **The City Hall's splendid Marble Hall contains statues of leading historic figures, including St David, Wales's patron saint (shown here), Owain Glyndŵr, Wales's last national leader, and Harri Tudur, the Welshman who became Henry VII, first of the Tudors.**

ABOVE **The architectural style of the National Museum of Wales mirrors that of its next-door neighbour, the City Hall.**

RIGHT **These figures in front of Mid Glamorgan County Hall represent navigation. Another group represents mining.**

The city centre

Cardiff's city centre is a well-balanced blend of old and new. On the one hand, it has been described as 'more than anything a Victorian city'; on the other, this embellished Victoriana rubs shoulders quite happily with newly developed modern shopping complexes.

The city's layout is compact and straightforward, ideally suited to exploration on foot. The two main shopping streets – pedestrianised Queen Street which runs from east to west, and the north–south St Mary Street – form an L-shape which partly encloses St David's Centre, Cardiff's largest shopping mall.

ABOVE **Cardiff's indoor market was constructed in cast iron and glass in 1891. Stalls on the ground floor and upstairs gallery, overlooked by the unusual old market office and clock tower, sell everything from Welsh lamb to clothes pegs.**

RIGHT **The market continues to attract the crowds. Its famous seafoods stall is a great favourite with shoppers.**

ABOVE **Queens Arcade, a new shopping centre based on one of the city's traditional canopied arcades, adopts a design which acknowledges the style of the original. On two levels, it connects with the large St David's Centre.**

RIGHT **Cardiff's many shopping arcades are a special feature of the city. The airy Castle Arcade, with its balcony, brightly coloured paintwork, mirrors and stained glass, is one of the finest.**

The city's Victorian face is at its best around The Hayes, an attractive open space close to the traditional covered market and many of the city's arcades. The exceptional concentration of glass-canopied Victorian and Edwardian shopping arcades – there are six in all, lined with a variety of speciality shops – adds a great deal of character to the city centre. The oldest is the Royal Arcade, dating from 1856, which links The Hayes to St Mary Street. Possibly the prettiest is the gleaming Castle Arcade which runs between Castle Street and High Street.

The modern equivalent of the old arcades are Cardiff's four covered shopping complexes. The first was the spacious St David's Centre which covers ten acres (4 ha) and the most recent is Queens Arcade which brings a fresh interpretation of the traditional 'arcade' theme to the city.

One of the most interesting Victorian buildings in the city centre is the Old Library, its fine south façade decorated with a bust of Athene, Goddess of Wisdom, and figures representing Calligraphy, Literature, Printing, Rhetoric and Study. It contains a crafts centre run by the Makers' Guild in Wales, a group of professional craftspeople.

ABOVE **Brains beer is a famous Cardiff institution. The family-owned brewery produces a traditional bitter beer and a distinctive dark ale for sale in pubs throughout Wales and the West Country.**

A walk

**Most of the city centre's majo
the castle, Victorian arcade
parklands and Civic Centre. T
hours but it ca**

To see the city's historic dockland
major redevelopment, you

START OUTSIDE the gatehouse of **Cardiff Castle** (pp. 6–9) (*above left*), cross the road and walk a short distance to the right along Castle Street to **Castle Arcade** (p. 13) (*above right*). Follow the covered arcade to High Street, cross the road and turn right and then left into Church Street, following it to the tall-towered **St John's Church** (p. 25) (*left*).

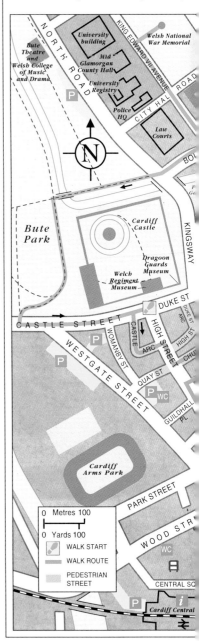

Turn right just before the church, heading along Trinity Street to the entrance to the **indoor market** (p. 12) (*below*) on the right. Walk through the covered Victorian market to emerge on St Mary Street, one of the city's main shopping streets. Turn left and then left again along Wharton Street to reach a pleasant open area overlooked by the **Old Library** crafts centre (p. 13).

Walk along The Hayes, turning right down **Royal Arcade** (p. 13) to emerge again on St Mary Street. Turn left and follow the street, which is lined with imposing Victorian buildings, to Mill Lane on the left, a junction marked by a statue of the second Marquess of Bute, the founder of modern Cardiff.

Mill Lane leads back to The Hayes; follow it and turn right into Hills Street, which has access to

Cardiff

...es can be seen on this walk –
...ern shopping complexes,
...walk takes about two to three
...be shortened.

...f the city centre, now undergoing
... a short bus or train trip.

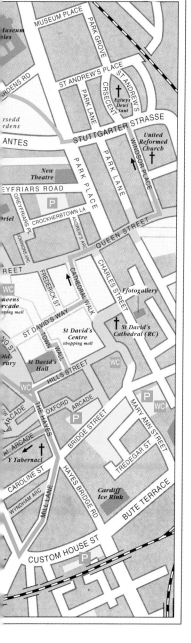

the **St David's Centre** modern shopping complex (*left*). Walk though this large centre to Queen Street, another main shopping street. Turn right along Queen Street and then left into Windsor Place (*below*), an attractive street of Georgian-style red-brick houses.

Turn left into Stuttgarter Strasse and continue into the Boulevard de Nantes – these streets are named after Cardiff's twinned German and French cities – to reach **Gorsedd Gardens** (p. 18) at the approach to the magnificent **Civic Centre** (pp. 10, 11). Directly in front of the gardens are two of the

Civic Centre's finest buildings – the **City Hall** (p. 10) (*below left*) and the **National Museum of Wales** (p. 11) (*below right*).

Walk across Gorsedd Gardens and into King Edward VII Avenue, between the City Hall the **Law Courts**, for a short

detour to **Alexandra Gardens** (pp. 18, 19) (*below*) at the heart of the Civic Centre. Return to the Boulevard de Nantes, turn right and cross North Road by the underpass to enter **Bute Park** (p. 18). Walk through this peaceful parkland behind the castle, turn left and continue to the Lodge. Here turn left into Castle Street and pass the **Animal Wall** (p. 6) on the left to return to the castle's gatehouse.

Maritime Cardiff

International singing star **Shirley Bassey** was born in the old docklands of Cardiff, which used to be known as Tiger Bay. The seventh child of an English mother and a Nigerian father, she began her professional career in the 1950s and by the early sixties had firmly established herself in America, performing regularly in Las Vegas. Her international fame was further boosted when she recorded the title songs to the James Bond films *Diamonds Are Forever*, *Moonraker* and *Goldfinger*.

Cardiff owes its existence – and its pre-eminence in Wales – to Butetown, the nineteenth-century docklands from which vast amounts of coal and iron were shipped to all parts of the world; in the nineteenth century Butetown *was* Cardiff. As the docks declined in this century, the emphasis shifted from the waterfront to modern Cardiff, a mile or so inland. Now the city is being reunited with its maritime heritage through the huge Cardiff Bay regeneration scheme. The 2,700-acre (1,092 ha) site will have a 500-acre (202 ha) freshwater lake and eight miles (13 km) of commercial and leisure developments along the waterfront.

Mount Stuart Square was the commercial heart of old Butetown. Its magnificent listed buildings – once the offices of coal and shipping merchants – have a grandeur that reflects the old docklands' great wealth and status. Dominating them

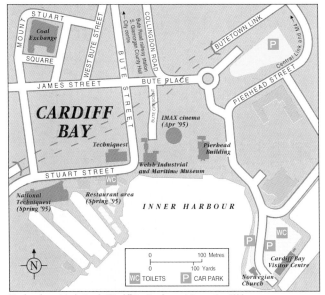

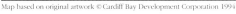
Map based on original artwork © Cardiff Bay Development Corporation 1994

ABOVE **Detail from the Cambrian Buildings just off Mount Stuart Square. The offices are noted for their ornate exterior carving.**

RIGHT **The clock in the Coal Exchange which reminded merchants of Cardiff's high-tide times. When coal trading was at its peak it was said that you could stand in the oak-panelled exchange and be surrounded by millionaire dealers.**

is the Coal Exchange, built along the lines of a Victorian stock exchange. The square is now becoming fashionable again as small companies, many connected with the film industry, have moved in.

All around Butetown a new Cardiff is taking shape. Along the waterfront past the ornate, red-brick Pierhead Building is the striking silver-tubed Cardiff Bay Visitor Centre, a futuristic structure displaying the plans which will take Cardiff Bay into the twenty-first century.

RIGHT The Pierhead Building's florid appearance has echoes of Cardiff Castle – no doubt because it was designed by William Frame, assistant to the great William Burges, the castle's architect. The building has remained virtually unchanged since 1896, when it was opened as offices for the Bute Dock Company. Sculptor Harvey Hood's bronze *Celtic Ring* is a recent addition to the waterfront, one of a number of sculptures here.

BELOW Looking like a grounded UFO, the Cardiff Bay Visitor Centre contains displays and models which explain the far-reaching plans to bring new life to the old docklands through the construction of a three-quarters of a mile (1.2 km) barrage across the mouth of the bay.

New offices and leisure developments are being built around the Inner Harbour, the bay's focal point, alongside Butetown's existing attractions of the Welsh Industrial and Maritime Museum and the Norwegian Church. One newcomer which is already very successful is National Techniquest, the largest 'hands-on' science centre in Britain. Future plans, which when realised will see the complete transformation of this area, include the construction of an opera house.

The waterfront can easily be visited from central Cardiff by frequent bus services and a 'shuttle' train from Queen Street station.

RIGHT The rejuvenation of Cardiff's waterfront has already achieved impressive results. The new South Glamorgan County Hall on Atlantic Wharf is in innovative 'pagoda' style with a Welsh slate roof.

Parks and gardens

BELOW **Bute Park, alongside Cardiff Castle and the River Taff, was landscaped by 'Capability' Brown in the late eighteenth century for the Bute family. Although only a few minutes' walk from the busy shopping streets and flanked by two of the city's main thoroughfares, it is an oasis of peace and tranquillity.**

Cardiff's green spaces reach right into the heart of the city. Within a stone's throw of the busy centre are extensive areas of peaceful parklands and gardens.

At the approach to the National Museum in the Civic Centre are the Gorsedd Gardens, a favourite lunchtime picnic area with office workers and shoppers. The gardens take their name from the *gorsedd*, the ceremonial circle of stones erected here to mark the holding of the National Eisteddfod at Cardiff in 1899.

The pretty Friary Gardens in front of the Law Courts are just across the road from an entrance to Bute Park. This large park, given to Cardiff along with the castle in 1947 by the Bute family, is a major landmark. It lies at the southern end of a green corridor of park and grassland – Sophia Gardens, Pontcanna Fields and Llandaff Fields – which extends for about two miles (3 km) along the banks of the River Taff to the pretty suburb of Llandaff.

The delightful Alexandra Gardens are at the heart of Cardiff's Civic Centre. Broad, tree-lined avenues,

colourful flowerbeds and neoclassical architecture provide the perfect backdrop to these formal gardens, which have the Welsh National War Memorial as their centrepiece.

Roath Park, a mile or so north-east of the centre, is another favourite green space, with the added attraction of a large boating lake which has a lighthouse as a memorial to Captain Scott, who sailed from Cardiff on his doomed mission to the South Pole. Other parks in Cardiff include Parc Cefn-onn and the Wenallt, both located on the northern edge of the city.

ABOVE LEFT **A statue of the third Marquess of Bute stands in Friary Gardens opposite the castle which he reconstructed.**

LEFT **The Welsh National War Memorial is in Alexandra Gardens at the heart of the Civic Centre. Unveiled in 1928, it consists of an elegant circular colonnade surrounding a sunken fountain and bronze sculpture of a soldier, sailor and airman.**

LEFT **Two-mile- (3 km) long Roath Park is in a residential part of Cardiff north-east of the city centre. It has a large boating lake with island sanctuaries for birdlife, as well as rose beds, formal and wild gardens, a sub- tropical plant house, children's play areas and a restored Victorian promenade and boathouse.**

Museums

Between them Cardiff's three major museums give visitors a complete insight into Wales and Welsh life – the origins of the country, its development over the ages, its environment and natural history, its rural traditions and its industrial importance.

Pride of place must go to the National Museum of Wales which stands imperiously in the Civic Centre. As well as being a repository of all things Welsh, the museum boasts a priceless collection of nineteenth-century French Impressionist art.

Works by some of the world's most renowned Impressionists – including Cézanne, Monet, Renoir and Van Gogh – are displayed in a series of new galleries. Welsh, British and other European paintings are also on show, together with collections of sculpture and ceramics including Rodin's bronze statue *The Kiss*.

The new galleries are part of a recently completed £26 million development programme which includes an 'Evolution of Wales' exhibition. This uses the latest techniques – robotics, film and special effects – to take visitors on a 4,600-million-year journey from the dawn of time to the last ice age 18,000 years ago.

Another new feature is the 'Natural History in Wales' exhibition which illustrates the marine and woodland environments of modern Wales. The museum also contains wide-ranging displays relating to archaeology, geology, history and natural history.

Wales of the nineteenth and early twentieth centuries is the inspiration

LEFT **The National Museum's spacious and impressive entrance hall lies beneath a domed ceiling 90 foot (27 m) high.**

BELOW **The dinosaur skeletons are some of the most spectacular exhibits in the National Museum's 'Evolution of Wales' display.**

LEFT A replica of Richard Trevithick's record-breaking locomotive can be seen at the Welsh Industrial and Maritime Museum. Contrary to popular opinion, Trevithick's engine was the first operational steam-powered locomotive. It ran on a tramway betwcen Merthyr Tydfil and Abercynon in 1804, over twenty years before George Stephenson's *Rocket*.

LEFT Engines which played such an important part in the industrial development of Wales are displayed in the Welsh Industrial and Maritime Museum's Hall of Power.

behind the Welsh Industrial and Maritime Museum in the old, but rapidly changing, docklands of Butetown. Machines of the Industrial Revolution used to power Wales's coalmines and ironworks are displayed in a large gallery beside Cardiff's historic waterfront. Starting with the simple waterwheel, the story moves on to the beam engine and many other types of steam engine, followed by gas engines and steam and gas turbines. Many of these engines are in full working order and are operated regularly. Due to open in 1995 on the site next to the museum is a globe-shaped IMAX virtual-reality cinema in which the audience is almost enveloped in the action.

The Rhyd-y-car cottages are part of a vast range of old buildings which have been re-erected at the Welsh Folk Museum. This small terrace, built in about 1800 to house workers of an iron-ore mine, comes from Merthyr Tydfil in the South Wales valleys.

RIGHT St Fagans Castle, within the grounds of the Welsh Folk Museum, dates from Norman times. The present house, built to a typical Elizabethan plan with an impressive long gallery, was built in 1580.

The picturesque village of St Fagans, on the western fringes of Cardiff and accessible by frequent bus services, is home to the Welsh Folk Museum. This open-air museum is a living record of the last few centuries in Wales. Buildings brought from all parts of the country have been painstakingly re-erected stone by stone, timber by timber, in an attractive parkland setting to create a comprehensive picture of Welsh life, traditions and culture.

The buildings include styles of farmhouse and cottage which range from the humble to the grand, a corn mill, tannery, smithy, barn, school, chapel, bakery, village shop, tollhouse, cockpit and a terrace of ironworkers' cottages. Many visitors spend an entire day at this multi-faceted museum, for in addition to the old buildings there is much more to see within this 100-acre (40 ha) site.

There are regular displays of traditional crafts, and a recreation of a Celtic village. A modern museum block is devoted to artefacts from Wales's domestic, cultural, social and rural life, with collections that include wooden lovespoons – intricately carved symbols of betrothal from the Wales of bygone times – and Welsh dressers. Also within the grounds is St Fagans Castle, a well-preserved

ABOVE **Llainfadyn cottage at the Welsh Folk Museum was brought from North Wales. The simple, single-roomed dwelling, built from rough boulders in 1762, was the home of a slate quarryman.**

LEFT **The First the Queen's Dragoon Guards Museum within Cardiff Castle has three galleries. The central gallery, spanning the regiment's history from 1850 to 1899, has a tableau depicting a mounted officer inspecting a sentry.**

Elizabethan manor house which stands in beautiful formal and terraced gardens.

Those interested in military memorabilia will find much to interest them in Cardiff Castle's two military museums. The Welch Regiment Museum spans 250 years of regimental history between 1719 and 1969, a period in which the regiment fought in the Battle of Waterloo, the Crimea, South Africa and the two world wars. The First the Queen's Dragoon Guards Museum contains collections from the regiment's foundation in 1685 to the present day, displayed in three main galleries.

Cardiff's smallest museum is the unusual little Museum of Magical Machines, based on kinetic sculptures, in the Old Library.

Religious sites

Cardiff's most famous place of worship stands about two miles (3 km) out of the city centre in the pretty suburb of Llandaff. The cathedral is the nucleus of a historic community which, despite Cardiff's urban expansion, still preserves its original village atmosphere and identity.

Hidden in a wooded hollow beside the River Taff, the cathedral stands on the site of a sixth-century church founded by the monastic leader St Teilo which served as a major religious centre for South Wales. The present cathedral was begun in the twelfth century by Bishop Urban and was complete by the fifteenth century, practically every style of medieval ecclesiastical architecture finding expression here.

Llandaff suffered serious neglect from the Middle Ages onwards, being described as 'a miserable poor village' with a ruined cathedral which was used as an ale-house and stables. Major restoration work began on the cathedral in the nineteenth century

BELOW **The uncompromisingly modernistic sculpture of *Christ in Majesty* by Sir Jacob Epstein dominates the interior of Llandaff Cathedral. It provoked fierce controversy when it was unveiled in the late 1950s.**

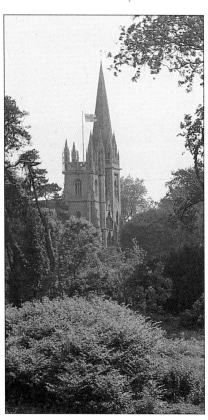

ABOVE **Llandaff, although now a suburb of Cardiff, preserves its original village atmosphere. At the end of its short shopping street a village green stands at the lip of a grassy hollow, the sheltered location of Llandaff Cathedral.**

but in 1941 a German landmine caused severe damage. Once again major rebuilding work took place, this time with two additions – the Welch Regiment Chapel, and Sir Jacob Epstein's striking *Christ in Majesty* sculpture in unpolished aluminium suspended on a parabolic arch of reinforced concrete above the nave.

The parish church of St John the Baptist stands somewhat incongruously among the new shopping precincts in the centre of Cardiff. With its soaring 130-foot (40 m) tower, St John's is a major historic landmark which features prominently in many old paintings and photographs of Cardiff.

Cardiff's Norwegian Church in Butetown is a testament to the international reputation which the city enjoyed as one of the world's great seaports. Originally a church and seamen's mission for Scandinavian sailors, it is now a cultural centre and coffee shop.

ABOVE St John's Church stands in the centre of Cardiff on a site which has seen Christian worship since Norman days, but the present building dates mainly from late medieval times. The Lady Chapel within contains monuments to two brothers, Sir William Herbert (died 1609), Keeper of Cardiff Castle, and Sir John Herbert (died 1617), private secretary to Elizabeth I and James I.

ABOVE The charming Norwegian Church on the waterfront overlooking Cardiff Bay was founded in 1867 but after falling into disrepair a century later was deconsecrated. It was rebuilt and resited in the early 1990s. Cardiff-born author Roald Dahl, whose Norwegian father made his fortune at Cardiff docks, was baptised here.

Entertainment

Cardiff's cultural and sporting life, a mix of traditional and cosmopolitan influences, is an accurate reflection of the city's character.

Think of Wales and you think of rugby. Think of rugby and you think of Cardiff Arms Park. This hallowed ground, familiar to rugby fans the world over, brings a special presence to the city because of its central location. Unlike many of Britain's famous rugby pitches, the Arms Park is within shouting distance of the city centre – with the consequence that all of Cardiff is caught up in the heady atmosphere of 'international' days.

RIGHT **Cardiff is the spiritual home of rugby. The world-famous Arms Park is a shrine to rugby fans from Aberystwyth and Auckland, Tonypandy and Toulouse.**

BELOW **The Cardiff Ice Rink, situated in the heart of the city, is popular with skaters of all abilities.**

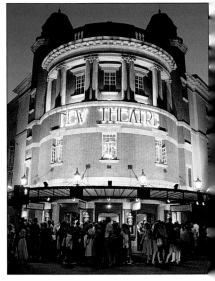

LEFT **Acoustically superb St David's Hall, the national concert hall of Wales, is one of Europe's most televised venues.**

ABOVE **The immaculately refurbished New Theatre is a much-loved stalwart of Cardiff's entertainments scene.**

Rugby is not Cardiff's only sporting passion. The Cardiff Devils, based at the Cardiff Ice Rink, also in the city centre, are one of Britain's top-ranking ice-hockey teams. Other sporting facilities around the city centre include the Welsh Institute of Sport, the Wales Empire Pool and the Cardiff Athletic Stadium.

Culture and the arts thrive in Cardiff. St David's Hall, Wales's national concert hall, is a popular and stylish venue for everything from comedy to classical music. The New Theatre, with its plush, Edwardian atmosphere, is the city's main home for drama, dance, and performances by the celebrated Welsh National Opera.

Contemporary theatre, art and cinema are well served by the progressive Chapter Arts Centre, while the Sherman Theatre's two auditoria offer a wide variety of live entertainment and films. The latest addition to the scene is the Cardiff International Arena, a huge multi-purpose complex which can stage major entertainment.

Cardiff's clubs and pubs support a flourishing jazz scene, and the city encourages quality street entertainment. Many festivals and special events enliven the entertainments scene. The Cardiff Festival, for example, held each September and October, presents literature, music, opera and theatre. And in July once every two years the city hosts the prestigious Cardiff Singer of the World Competition which has uncovered great new talents.

ABOVE **Welsh National Opera, a company of international repute, is based in Cardiff. Performances are held in the New Theatre, though plans are afoot to construct a new opera house as part of the wholesale redevelopment of Cardiff's waterfront. The above scene is from Rossini's** *The Barber of Seville*.

LEFT **Street entertainers are a common sight in Cardiff. The city's efforts to encourage quality entertainment are highlighted during the International Festival of Street Entertainment which is held in Cardiff each year.**

Further information

All details are correct at the time of writing but please confirm opening times before making a visit.

ABOVE **The decorative Pierhead Building is close to the Cardiff Bay Visitor Centre on the redeveloped waterfront.**

Cardiff Bay Visitor Centre

Space-age design – a silver tube containing displays of the massive redevelopments taking place at Cardiff Bay.
On the Inner Harbour waterfront in Butetown (Tel: 01222 463833). Open Mon–Fri 9.30–4.30, Sat, Sun and bank hols 10.30–5. Admission free.

Cardiff Castle

Fascinating historic site – a Roman fort, Norman keep and Victorian mansion – which reflects the fortunes of the city. Also contains two regimental museums (see separate entries).
Castle Street/Duke Street (Tel: 01222 822083). Open daily May–Sept 10–6; Mar, Apr and Oct 10–5; Nov–Feb 10–4.30. Admission charge.

Cardiff City Hall

Elegant centrepiece of Cardiff's Civic Centre. Marble Hall with 'Heroes of Wales' statues open to the public.

Civic Centre (Tel: 01222 822000). Open Mon–Fri 9–5. Admission free.

Caerphilly Castle

Vast medieval fortress and complex water defences rivalling Windsor in size. One of Britain's most underrated historic sites.
In Caerphilly, 7 miles (11 km) north of Cardiff (Tel: 01222 883143). Open late Mar–late Oct daily 9.30–6.30; late Oct–late Mar Mon–Sat 9.30–4, Sun 11–4. Admission charge.

Castell Coch

Romantic 'Sleeping Beauty' castle on steep, wooded hillside near Cardiff. A nineteenth-century creation and companion-piece to Cardiff Castle, designed by William Burges for the third Marquess of Bute.
At Tongwynlais 5 miles (8 km) north-west of city centre (Tel: 01222 810101). Open late Mar–late Oct daily 9.30–6.30; late Oct–late Mar Mon–Sat 9.30–4, Sun 11–4. Admission charge.

ABOVE **Mighty Caerphilly Castle, with its extensive water defences, is an outstanding example of medieval military architecture.**

Ffotogallery

Wales's leading gallery for contemporary photographic work of the highest quality. Changing exhibitions, specialist bookshop.
31 Charles Street (Tel: 01222 341667). Open Tue–Sat 10–5.30. Admission free.

First the Queen's Dragoon Guards Museum

Imaginatively presented military memorabilia from the Cavalry Regiment of Wales.
See Cardiff Castle.

BELOW **Fairytale Castell Coch at Tongwynlais was built as a country retreat for the third Marquess of Bute.**